8 00

# CHRIST IN POETRY

# Christ in Poetry

## AN ANTHOLOGY

### COMPILED AND EDITED BY

### THOMAS CURTIS CLARK

### AND

### HAZEL DAVIS CLARK

ASSOCIATION PRESS

NEW YORK

55

Printed in the United States of America
American Book—Stratford Press, Inc.

# PREFACE

Brought up in the home of a minister, I early learned the story of Christ. The Christ my father preached was no mystical being, far from our weak humanity. He was the Christ so vividly portrayed in the Gospels, the close Friend, the ministering Servant; One who spent his later years talking with people who had problems—the lame and halt, lonely, bewildered men and women; One who found joy in taking little children into his arms. The Christ who afforded a subject for the Nicene and Athanasian dogmatists had little place in my father's preaching. He seldom mentioned the creeds, and I do not remember his preaching any sermons on the Trinity as such; for my minister-father was not a product of any school of theology. He had been a carpenter, and his later education was derived from a "secular" university. But he did preach about "the Man Christ Jesus,"

> the lord of our hearts, of our homes,
> Of our hopes, our prayers, our needs;
> The brother of want and blame,
> The lover of women and men,
> With a love that puts to shame
> All passions of human ken. . . .

It is largely this friendly, sympathetic Christ, "the lover of women and men"—the Christ my father preached—who is portrayed in this book. The poets of recent decades have seen Christ in the same way; and the poets are excellent interpreters of Christ, who also was a poet.

Some thirty years ago there appeared an anthology entitled *Christ in the Poetry of Today*. It had been assembled by Martha Foote Crow. This book had a worthy purpose: to reveal how since the turn of the century Christ had become a favorite theme for poetic treatment. The compiler found delight in proving concretely that a veritable tide of good poetry about Christ was then receiving publication. Her satisfaction with this new development was amply justified. Moreover, the fact that the bulk of this new poetry portrayed not "the Christ of our subtle creeds," but "the lover of women and men," brought intense satisfaction to this deep-seeing anthologist.

The years that have gone their way since the publication of *Christ in the Poetry of Today* have witnessed an ever increasing number of poems on the Christ theme. These poems would perhaps not be useful to any modern "Council of Nicaea"; for they are close to life, they have the human touch, they see Christ as the Man Christ Jesus.

As poetry editor for the *Christian Century* for more than a quarter-century, I have had the privilege of passing editorially on much of the better religious poetry that has been written during the exciting years since the First World War. We have included in this anthology the best of these *Christian Century* poems that portray "the Christ who enters our door," the Christ who said "I am among you as one that serveth" and "I have called you friends."

> The healing of his seamless dress
>     Is by our beds of pain;
> We touch him in life's throng and press,
>     And we are whole again.

But this is not simply a gathering together of poems about Christ written during the present century. The book certainly gains significance by the inclusion of standard poems by Browning, Tennyson, Arnold, Longfellow, Lowell, Whittier, and other writers of earlier days. Even old John Donne is here.

The philosopher Fichte had this to say of the subject of our book: "Till the end of time all the sensible will bow low before this Jesus of Nazareth, and will humbly acknowledge the exceeding glory of this great phenomenon. His followers are nations and generations. Jesus did more than all the philosophers in bringing heavenly morality into the hearts and homes of common men. To the end of time, all wise and intelligent men must bow reverently before Jesus; and the more wise, intelligent, they are, the more humbly will they recognize the exceeding nobleness of this great and glorious manifestation of the Divine Life."

To the tributes of prophets and apostles, of philosophers and sages, has now been added the testimony of the poets; and the more recent singers claim a place in this great congregation of worshipers. They have told of the Man Christ Jesus, for they feel that his glorious humanity may have been overlooked. Having seen the friendly, human Christ through their rapt eyes, we shall certainly go forward to a still higher view: we shall see him as our Divine Lord and Saviour. How else can his human superiority be explained?

THOMAS CURTIS CLARK

*Bellwood, Illinois*
*January, 1952*

# ACKNOWLEDGMENTS

Acknowledgment is hereby gratefully made of the generous co-operation of both contributing poets and publishers in the compilation of this anthology. The compilers have made every effort to trace the ownership of all copyrighted poems. To the best of their knowledge they have secured all necessary permissions from authors or their authorized agents, or from both. Should there be a question regarding the use of any poem, regret is expressed for unconscious error.

So far as possible the styling—punctuation, spelling, capitalization, and so forth—conforms to that found in original standard versions. This explains the variations in the text of the anthology.

Permission has been received, either from the poets or from their estates, for the inclusion of poems by the following authors: Phoebe Smith Bachelder, Dorothy Scott Ballard, Mary Dickerson Bangham, Katharine Lee Bates, Gertrude Ryder Bennett, Carl John Bostelmann, Dwight Bradley, Verne Bright, Louise Upham Brooks, William E. Brooks, Earl Bigelow Brown, Aubert Edgar Bruce, Loren W. Burch, Helen M. Burgess, William Capell, George W. Carlin, Aline Badger Carter, Ralph Cheyney, Leslie Savage Clark, Sarah N. Cleghorn, Catherine Cate Coblentz, Stanton A. Coblentz, Ernest Cadman Colwell, Allen Eastman Cross, Donald Earl Edwards, Franklin D. Elmer, Jr., Harold E. Fey, Mahlon Leonard Fisher, Natalie Flohr, Florence Kiper Frank, Herbert D. Gallaudet, Winfred Ernest Garrison, Esther Lloyd Hagg, Molly Anderson Haley, Mary Hallet,

Gertrude Hanson, Georgia Harkness, Una W. Harsen, Sara Henderson Hay, Daniel Henderson, George Edward Hoffman, William H. Hudnut, Jr., Daniel Hughes, Harry Kemp, Raymond Kresensky, Winifred Stoddard LeBar, Mary Sinton Leitch, Elinor Lennen, Lilith Lorraine, Arthur R. Macdougall, Jr., Clyde McGee, Edwin Markham, Earl Marlatt, Beulah May, Lloyd Frank Merrell, Edith Mirick, John Richard Moreland, Ida Norton Munson, John Oxenham, Myriam Page, J. R. Perkins, Edith Lovejoy Pierce, J. Franklin Pineo, Kenneth W. Porter, Edwin McNeill Poteat, Winnie Lynch Rockett, E. Merrill Root, Mary Ross, Leila Avery Rothenburger, Rolland W. Schloerb, Walter Shea, Sheldon Shepard, Margaret Evelyn Singleton, William L. Stidger, William J. Suckow, Ruby Weyburn Tobias, Lucia Trent, Elizabeth Waddell, Louise Webster, Carl S. Weist, Robert Whitaker.

Sincere thanks are due the following publishers for granting permission to use poems by the authors indicated:

W. B. Conkey Company: poem by Ella Wheeler Wilcox.

Harper and Brothers: poems by G. A. Studdert-Kennedy.

Houghton Mifflin Company: poems by Gilder, Longfellow, Lowell, and Whittier from their *Complete Poetical Works*.

Bruce Humphries, Inc.: poems by Ida Norton Munson.

The Macmillan Company: poems by Matthew Arnold, Robert Browning, and Alfred Tennyson from their *Collected Works*.

Charles Scribner's Sons: excerpt from "The Toiling of Felix," reprinted from *The Poems of Henry van Dyke*; copyright 1911 by Charles Scribner's Sons, 1939 by Tertius van Dyke; used by permission of the publishers.

The *Christian Century*, in which publication many of the poems included first appeared.

THE COMPILERS

# Contents

xiii

# Contents

## IN NAZARETH

## THE MAN CHRIST JESUS

# Contents

## THE WAY OF THE CROSS

# Contents

# Contents

## COME, FOLLOW ME

# Contents

## THE CONTINUING CHRIST

# Contents xxvii

## THE TRIUMPHANT CHRIST

# Contents xxxi

*Behold Him now as He comes!*
  *Not the Christ of our subtle creeds,*
*But the Light of our hearts and our*
    *homes,*
  *Our hopes, our fears, our needs,*
*The brother of want and blame,*
  *The lover of women and men,*
*With a love that puts to shame*
  *All passions of mortal ken....*

*Ah, no, thou life of the heart,*
*Never shalt thou depart!*
*Not till the heaven of God*
*Shall lighten each human clod;*
*Not till the world shall climb*
*To the height serene, sublime,*
*Shall the Christ who enters our door*
*Pass to return no more.*

RICHARD WATSON GILDER

*He shall not desert us.*

# Nativity

# *Nativity*

### From "In Memoriam"

The time draws near the birth of Christ.
  The moon is hid, the night is still;
  The Christmas bells from hill to hill
Answer each other in the mist.

Four voices of four hamlets round,
  From far and near, on mead and moor,
  Swell out and fail, as if a door
Were shut between me and the sound;

Each voice four changes on the wind,
  That now dilate, and now decrease,
  Peace and goodwill, goodwill and peace,
Peace and goodwill, to all mankind.
ALFRED TENNYSON

## Annunciation Night

It was night in the village of Nazareth,
   But the dark, like the dusk of a blessed death,
Was pierced with splendor and voices tender,
   And the breeze died down to a zephyr's breath.

Stars sang as they swung in their ordered courses
   And planets circling around the sun;
And all life stirred at its inmost sources
   With sense of the Wonder on earth begun.

But the little fair Virgin of Nazareth slept,
   Dreaming the touch of the hand of her Child,
And angels above her their vigil kept,
   And oft in her sleep she tenderly smiled.

For God to his own Creation knit
   His life and hers not a breath apart;
While Heav'n was athrill at the thought of it—
   The Hope of the Worlds hidden under her heart!

              KATHERINE E. CONWAY

## Before the Paling of the Stars

Before the paling of the stars,
   Before the winter morn,
Before the earliest cockcrow,
   Jesus Christ was born:

Born in a stable,
  Cradled in a manger,
In the world his hands had made
  Born a stranger.

Priest and king lay fast asleep
  In Jerusalem,
Young and old lay fast asleep
  In crowded Bethlehem;
Saint and Angel, ox and ass,
  Kept a watch together
Before the Christmas daybreak
  In the winter weather.

Jesus on his mother's breast
  In the stable cold,
Spotless Lamb of God was he,
  Shepherd of the fold:
Let us kneel with Mary maid,
  With Joseph bent and hoary,
With Saint and Angel, ox and ass,
  To hail the King of Glory.
            CHRISTINA G. ROSSETTI


## From "Hamlet"

Some say that ever 'gainst that season comes
Wherein our Saviour's birth is celebrated,
The bird of dawning singeth all night long:
And then, they say, no spirit can walk abroad;
The nights are wholesome; then no planets strike,

No fairy takes, nor witch hath power to charm;
So hallow'd and so gracious is the time.

WILLIAM SHAKESPEARE

## The Path of the Stars

Down through the spheres that chant the Name of One
  Who is the Law of Beauty and of Light
  He came, and as He came the waiting Night
Shook with gladness of a Day begun;
And as He came, He said: Thy Will be Done
  On Earth; and all His vibrant Words were white
  And glistering with silver, and their might
Was of the glory of a rising sun.
Unto the Stars sang out His Living Words
  White and with silver, and their rhythmic sound
    Was a mighty symphony unfurled;
And back from out the Stars like homing birds
  They fell in love upon the sleeping ground
    And were forever in a wakened world.

THOMAS S. JONES, JR.

## From "A Hymn of the Nativity"

Welcome to our wondering sight,
  Eternity shut in a span!
Summer in winter! Day in night!
  Heaven in earth! and God in man!
Great little one, whose glorious birth
Lifts earth to Heaven, stoops Heaven to earth.

RICHARD CRASHAW

### From "Saint Paul"

Lo! as some venturer, from his stars receiving
  Promise and presage of sublime emprise,
Wears evermore the seal of his believing
  Deep in the dark of solitary eyes,

So even I, and with a pang more thrilling,
  So even I, and with a hope more sweet,
Yearn for the sign, O Christ, of Thy fulfilling,
  Faint for the flaming of Thine advent feet.

FREDERICK W. H. MYERS

### The Kings of the East

The Kings of the East are riding
  Tonight to Bethlehem.
The sunset glows dividing,
The Kings of the East are riding;
A star their journey guiding,
  Gleaming with gold and gem
The Kings of the East are riding
  Tonight to Bethlehem.

.     .     .     .     .     .

There beams above a manger
  The child-face of a star;
Amid the stars a stranger,
It beams above a manger;

What means this ether-ranger
    To pause where poor folk are?
There beams above a manger
    The child-face of a star.
          KATHARINE LEE BATES

### The Three Wise Men

#### *The First*

I came from Tigris' sandy plain
    Where I beheld the wondrous star;
With my slow-creeping camel train
    I nightly followed it afar.

#### *The Second*

I came from Persia's table-land
    That lies beyond the Syrian dawn;
A candle in an angel's hand
    It seemed, before the stars had gone.

#### *The Third*

And I, 'mid mountains heavenward piled,
    I saw the star that led them west;
I, too, with them would seek the Child.
    I, too, would make the Holy Quest.

#### *The Three*

We asked in great Jerusalem,
    But none could tell us of his birth,

And then to little Bethlehem
We came—the least of all the earth.

There came we to our journey's goal;
No farther had we need to roam;
There was a home for every soul
Where Christ himself could find no home.

JOHN FINLEY

## Three Gifts

Gold and frankincense and myrrh,
Lord, they brought to Thee;
And myrrh was death, and incense prayer,
And gold was victory.
But first is last as last was first;
The myrrh they gave Thee in Thy thirst
Upon the tree.
And through the solemn centuries
The prayers of saints have risen
From hearth and chancel, crypt and tomb,
From pyre and from prison.
Now never was the mystic power
Of the gold fulfilled;
Yet draweth on the mighty hour
By the Father willed
When every knee shall bow to him
Who on the cross was lift,
And every tongue acclaim him king;
This is the golden gift.

EDWARD JUDSON HANNA

## Three Wise Kings

To Bethlehem town in the long ago
Three Kings of the East came riding;
Over the plains where the hot sands glow,
And over the mountains deep in snow,
Seeking the King in the manger low—
Three Kings of the East a-riding.

To the inn they came, to the common room,
And they bowed them low before him;
And spices and gold and rare perfume
They piled at his feet in the gathering gloom,
But the Christ-Child's eyes lit up the room,
As he smiled at the gray heads o'er him.

Then into the night to their lands afar,
The bells on their camels ringing,
They took their way where the wide plains are;
But gone from the sky was the Christmas star,
And strangely gone were the fears that mar,
While peace in their hearts was singing.

And ever as dawns the Christmas Day,
The worn old world goes faring,
Seeking the place where the young Child lay,
Where the Kings of the East bowed low to pray,
And peace was born to abide alway,
In hearts that were long despairing.

WILLIAM E. BROOKS

### Gifts

Three kings there were from Orient who came,
Led by a star with strange, compelling flame,
        A Prince's sign;
And shepherds, too, followed its beckoning light,
        Godhood benign!
That blessed the givers of the royal gold,
But smiled upon the lambkin from the fold.

We, too, may bring our frankincense and myrrh,
And pay our tribute there, as though we were
        Of kingly birth;
But 'tis not gifts like these that he doth prize
So much as those which come in lowlier wise
        From the poor of earth,
Who having naught of gold or treasure-trove
Bring that of which they have the chiefest, *love*.

                        HELEN WIEAND COLE

### Magi

How brief that holy hour they knew
    When, traveling far,
They knelt to offer gold and myrrh
    Beneath a star!

How strange and sad that time should tell
    No more of them,

Nor if they followed him they sought
In Bethlehem!
LESLIE SAVAGE CLARK

### A Different Way

Wise men, indeed, to know a new-born star
Would be the herald of a king! Wise men,
To watch in readiness and travel far
To seek a light beyond their fellows' ken!
At star-bathed stable to rejoice, and when
They saw the Babe, to kneel and humbly lay
Their richest gifts of gold, of myrrh; and then
To travel back, dream-told, another way!

Ah, rare and wondrous wisdom—in our day
To read God's portents and to find his key!
Sweet manger Baby, to Thy tender sway
We yield all pride, all knowledge—gifts for Thee.
We worship in the radiance of Thy face,
And rise, a different way of life to trace.
ESTHER LLOYD HAGG

### The Bethlehem Road

Past the closed portals of earthly kings,
And by crowded inns it lies—
The Bethlehem road—so near, so sure,
Made plain under starlit skies;

The road that the songs of angels laid,
And marked by footprints the shepherds made.

The Bethlehem road that the Wise Men knew
    Still sheds its radiant light
For eyes that weep, for hearts that mourn,
    In earth's broken homes tonight.
And close to the sleepless sufferer's bed
Is the Christ-Child's love and comfort spread.

And the Bethlehem road—it winds afar,
    Nor loses its constant way;
So loved ones here, or loved ones there,
    Are safe on its path alway.
For ever upon its course there lies
The blessed hope from the Christ-Child's eyes.

IDA NORTON MUNSON

## Caravans

The shaggy camels kneel upon the sand
As skies grow red above the setting sun.
Beside their patient beasts the Wise Men stand
With gifts of incense, gold and myrrh for One
Who lies beneath the new-found star. Four beams
Shoot out. The star appears to hang upon
A cross of fire. The turbaned heads bear dreams
Of peace while swaying camels stride toward dawn.

Those beasts are desert dust. Their progeny
Who trail the starry plane are bearing now
Dark gifts of war. A fleeting imagery

Of power is borne beneath the helmet's brow.
But yet the ancient dream shall never cease
While other caravans of mind bear peace.

EMILY PATTERSON

## Peace on Earth

Shepherds there were who in the fields by night
Kept watch, not wisting that a chorus bright
Of angels would to them the news convey—
The dawning of the world's most potent day.

Countless the nights of darkness and of fear
The world has watched through, but the message clear
Of prophets, martyrs, saints and poets brought
The healing word for which it blindly sought.

Visions from God—through men must come the word,
Till the whole earth to action deeply stirred
From war and dread and hatred wins release,
And hails once more as King the Prince of Peace.

HELEN WIEAND COLE

## The Shepherd Speaks

Out of the midnight sky a great dawn broke,
And a voice singing flooded us with song.
In David's city was He born, it sang,
A Saviour, Christ the Lord. Then while I sat

Shivering with the thrill of that great cry,
A mighty choir a thousandfold more sweet
Suddenly sang, Glory to God, and Peace—
Peace on the earth; my heart, almost unnerved
By that swift loveliness, would hardly beat.
Speechless we waited till the accustomed night
Gave us no promise more of sweet surprise;
Then scrambling to our feet, without a word
We started through the fields to find the Child.

JOHN ERSKINE

## A Christmas Carol

"What means this glory 'round our feet,"
  The Magi mused, "more bright than morn?"
And voices chanted clear and sweet,
  "Today the Prince of Peace is born!"

"What means that star," the shepherds said,
  "That brightens through the rocky glen?"
And angels, answering overhead,
  Sang, "Peace on earth, good-will to men!"

'Tis eighteen hundred years and more
  Since those sweet oracles were dumb;
We wait for him, like them of yore;
  Alas, he seems so slow to come.

But it was said in words of gold,
  No time or sorrow e'er shall dim,

That little children might be bold
  In perfect trust to come to Him.

All 'round about our feet shall shine
  A light like that the wise men saw,
If we our willing hearts incline
  To that sweet Life which is the Law.

So shall we learn to understand
  The simple faith of shepherds then,
And, kindly clasping hand in hand,
  Sing, "Peace on earth, good-will to men."

For they who to their childhood cling,
  But keep their natures fresh as morn,
Once more shall hear the angels sing,
  "Today the Prince of Peace is born!"
                    JAMES RUSSELL LOWELL

### The Light of Bethlehem

'Tis Christmas night! The snow,
  A flock unnumbered, lies:
The old Judean stars, aglow,
  Keep watch within the skies.

An icy stillness holds
  The pulses of the night:
A deeper mystery infolds
  The wondering hosts of light.

Till, lo, with reverence pale
    That dims each diadem,
The lordliest, earthward bending, hail
    The light of Bethlehem!

JOHN BANISTER TABB

## No Room

Once when they gathered long ago
    At taxing time, in David's town,
The village inn was crowded so
    With those who laid large monies down,
There was no room except a stall
    Back yonder where the cattle were,
When Mary came, the blest of all—
    No room, though God had chosen her.

And what if in these taxing times,
    Our land, the whole world's inn of old,
Is crowded so with men whose crimes
    Have filled their pilfering palms with gold,
And with their slavish retinues
    Of serving maids and serving men—
What if, when God bends low to choose,
    His choice shall find no room again?

ROBERT WHITAKER

### The Father

O Joseph, of the holy family least,
  A just man art thou called, and all the rest
Of flaw and virtue in thy homely life
  Is left unnamed, to be inferred or guessed.

But who can doubt thy warmth of heart, thy grace
  Of spirit wise, or who shall think it odd
To hold thee great? When Jesus spoke to heaven,
  "My Father" was the name he gave to God.

DOROTHY SCOTT BALLARD

### "Mary Pondered All These Things"

Mother Mary's mind—
A repository—
Cherished every kind
Of event and story.
She remembered what
Joseph soon forgot.

Quite incredible
How she could recall
Word and miracle,
Pain and passion! All
Through the days she pondered
In her heart, and wondered.

Mothers still, it seems,
Keep their hearts like Mary—
Full of words and dreams—
Like a reliquary.
Men like Joseph yet
Easily forget.
    EDWIN MCNEILL POTEAT

## Annunciation to All Women

The angel came with lilies three,
Said, Mary, hear, these things shall be:
You shall bear a child in pain,
Nurture him through sun and rain.
He shall learn his father's trade,
Wood planed smooth and straightly laid.
But when he becomes a man
He must choose after God's plan,
Either to nail another's tree,     condemn all
Or hang, for all, on Calvary.     u hear all sin
    AGNES C. FOOTE

## Offering

Did Mary know when the Wise Men laid
    Myrrh at his little feet
Of the tragic hour when women would bring
    Myrrh for his winding sheet?
    LESLIE SAVAGE CLARK

## That Holy Thing

They all were looking for a king
    To slay their foes and lift them high;
Thou cam'st, a little baby thing
    That made a woman cry.

O Son of Man, to right my lot
    Naught but Thy presence can avail;
Yet on the road Thy wheels are not,
    Nor on the sea Thy sail!

My how or when Thou wilt not heed,
    But come down Thine own secret stair,
That Thou may'st answer all my need—
    Yea, every bygone prayer.
                GEORGE MacDONALD

## God With Us

There were three lights that night:
The star above the darkness, crystal fair,
The foremost angel's garment flaming white,
        The baby's circled hair.

Three sounds upon the hill:
A sudden song; low drawn, a woman's sigh;
And, when the midnight deepened gray and chill,
        A little, little cry.

Three woes: a witless lamb
Lost from the scattered flock; its mother grieving;
The long, deep slumber of the townfolk—blind
      And deaf and unbelieving.

Three wonders: dark-browed kings
Riding from far; young shepherds' lifted faces;
The silver beauty raining from the star
      On Bethlehem's dark places.

There were Faith, Hope and Love:
Faith that had known, Hope that waited well,
Love that had wrought; and in their trembling midst,
      Immanuel!

NANCY BYRD TURNER

## Come, Holy Babe!

Did Bethlehem's stable loathe
Its drab, dull stone?
And did the oxen sense their common lot?
The hay its coarse inadequacy?
The earth-pressed floor, unworthiness?

My heart is shabby, too:
Come, Manger Light!
Make my dull spirit glow
*This* Silent Night!

MARY DICKERSON BANGHAM

### There's a Song in the Air!

There's a song in the air!
   There's a star in the sky!
There's a mother's deep prayer
   And a baby's low cry!
And the star rains its fire while the beautiful sing,
For the manger of Bethlehem cradles a King!

There's a tumult of joy
   O'er the wonderful birth,
For the Virgin's sweet boy
   Is the Lord of the earth.
Ay! the star rains its fire while the beautiful sing,
For the manger of Bethlehem cradles a King!

In the light of that star
   Lie the ages impearled;
And that song from afar
   Has swept over the world.
Every hearth is aflame, and the beautiful sing
In the homes of the nations that Jesus is King.

We rejoice in the light,
   And we echo the song
That comes down through the night
   From the heavenly throng.
Ay! we shout to the lovely evangel they bring,
And we greet in his cradle our Saviour and King!

JOSIAH GILBERT HOLLAND

## Unto Us a Son Is Given

Given, not lent,
And not withdrawn—once sent,
This Infant of mankind, this One,
Is still the little welcome Son.

New every year,
New born and newly dear, *Jn 3; 3*
He comes with tidings and a song,
The ages long, the ages long;

Even as the cold
Keen winter grows not old,
As childhood is so fresh, foreseen,
And spring in the familiar green.

Sudden as sweet
Come the expected feet.
All joy is young, and new all art,
And He, too, Whom we have by heart.

ALICE MEYNELL

## From "A Christmas Antiphone"

Thou whose birth on earth
    Angels sang to men,
While thy stars made mirth,
    This day born again.

As this night was bright
  With thy cradle-ray,
Very light of light,
Turn the wild world's night
  To Thy perfect day.
          A. C. SWINBURNE


### Incarnate Love

Love came down at Christmas,
  Love all lovely, Love Divine;
Love was born at Christmas,
  Star and Angels gave the sign.

Worship we the Godhead,
  Love incarnate, Love Divine;
Worship we our Jesus:
  But wherewith for sacred sign?

Love shall be our token,
  Love be yours and Love be mine,
Love to God and all men,
  Love for plea and gift and sign.
          CHRISTINA G. ROSSETTI


### Christmas Rose

From the ageless garden plot of Time he came,
To flower from the mighty Gardener's seed,
Full proof that Goodness is the garden soil.

Across eternity and earth his name
In blooms of herald-song replied to need,
And Love succeeded cultivation's toil.
                    MARGARET EVELYN SINGLETON


## Christmas

As shadows cast by cloud and sun
    Flit o'er the summer grass,
So, in thy sight, Almighty One,
    Earth's generations pass.
And as the years, an endless host,
    Come swiftly pressing on,
The brightest names that earth can boast
    Just glisten and are gone.

Yet doth the star of Bethlehem shed
    A luster pure and sweet:
And still it leads, as once it led,
    To the Messiah's feet.
O Father, may that holy star
    Grow every year more bright,
And send its glorious beams afar
    To fill the world with light.
                    WILLIAM CULLEN BRYANT

### The Star

We know not through what trackless space of night,
Nor from what realms it brought the radiant light,
What deserts, seas, or gardens felt its ray,
Before its beams touched where the Christ-Child lay.

Men may not sight it, measure its vast swing,
Nor time its balance like a temporal thing;
Yet close, at Christmas, gleams the age-old sign
Of Bethlehem's Star, above your heart and mine.

IDA NORTON MUNSON

### The Nativity

Here is "the hinge of history"—the hour
Wherefrom the years recede, the years advance—
The night when Love has victory over Power.

A new-born child beneath a mother's glance,
God the Creator is made manifest,
Born of his creature, flesh of circumstance.

Here, petal-soft against his mother's breast,
He lies who made the sun to be his rose;
Here he who strews the lightnings lies at rest!

O little hands that fold the falling snows!
O baby hands that buoy the nightingale!
How can your fingers sleep in such repose?

And must you, O soft baby feet, rescale
The height of Heaven on the driven nail?

E. MERRILL ROOT

## This Holy Night

God, let our sons this Holy Night,
Above war's fearful din,
For one trust-bringing moment glimpse
A small Judean Inn,
Sweet Mary, and the Holy Child,
A Star, a manger-bed;
And hush war's clamor till our sons
Hear Angel-Song instead.

GERTRUDE HANSON

## We Have Seen His Star in the East

"We have seen his star in the East,"
In the East where it first stood still,
We have heard the song of the angel throng,
"And on earth peace, good will!"
But the little lights confuse,
The nearer sounds obsess,
And our hearts withhold from the Lord of Love
The lives he would use and bless.

"We have seen his star in the East,"
His shining dream of the good,

When men shall claim in the Father's name
   Their right to brotherhood.
O little lights, grow dim,
   O nearer sounds, be still,
While our hearts remember Bethlehem,
   And a cross on a far green hill!

MOLLY ANDERSON HALEY

## A Christmas Prayer

We open here our treasures and our gifts;
And some of it is gold,
And some is frankincense,
And some is myrrh;
For some has come from plenty,
Some from joy,
And some from deepest sorrow of the soul.
But Thou, O God, dost know the gift is love,
Our pledge of peace, our promise of good-will.
Accept the gift and all the life we bring.

HERBERT H. HINES

## Hush, All Ye Sounds of War

Hush, all ye sounds of war,
Ye nations all be still,
A voice of heav'nly joy steals over vale and hill,
O hear the angels sing the captive world's release,
This day is born in Bethlehem the Prince of Peace.

No more divided be,
Ye families of men,
Old enmity forget, old friendship knit again,
In the new year of God let brothers' love increase,
This day is born in Bethlehem the Prince of Peace.

WILLIAM H. DRAPER

## Eternal Christmas

In the pure soul, although it sing or pray,
The Christ is born anew from day to day;
The life that knoweth him shall bide apart
And keep eternal Christmas in the heart.

ELIZABETH STUART PHELPS

## The Heart Is Bethlehem

I dyed my rooms in candle glow,
Hung holly wreaths and mistletoe,
And in the passing lure of them
Forgot the heart is *Bethlehem*.
"With tinsel glory I trimmed a tree
But I forgot the heart of me—"
That it is there the Christ must stay
When he comes in on Christmas Day.

I made no place for the Christ-Child then ...
O that he pass this way again!

GERTRUDE HANSON

## I Must Light a Candle

I must light a glowing candle
For sweet Mary's Infant child—
The streets are ice, the winds blow wild,
      Winds blow wild.

I must light a glowing candle
For the gentle Teacher, One
Friendless, homeless, God's own Son,
      God's own Son.

I must light a glowing candle
For his cross-racked agony—
My heart-glow lighted thankfully,
      Thankfully.

GERTRUDE HANSON

## December Twenty-fourth

Tomorrow you are born again
    Who died so many times.
Do you like the candle-light,
    Do you like the chimes?

Do you stop to wonder
    Why men never see
How very closely Bethlehem
    Approaches Calvary?

ELEANOR SLATER

### Day Dawn of the Heart

*good*

'Tis not enough that Christ was born
   Beneath the star that shone,
And earth was set that holy morn
   Within a golden zone.
He must be born within the heart
   Before he finds his throne,
And brings the day of love and good,
The reign of Christlike brotherhood.

MARY T. LATHROP

### In Thine Own Heart

Though Christ a thousand times
   In Bethlehem be born,
If he's not born in thee
   Thy soul is still forlorn.
The cross on Golgotha
   Will never save thy soul,
The cross in thine own heart
   Alone can make thee whole.

*when Christ is My Saviour.*

ANGELUS SILESIUS

### Christmas Blessing

Father, send us for this meal
   An unexpected guest,
A child perhaps from war-wracked town,
   With horror clutching at its breast.

Let us read, in hungering eyes,
   A prayer, sharp as any sword,
That the feast upon our table
   May serve a living Lord.
                FRANKLIN D. ELMER, JR.

### The Christmas Tree

If Christ could ever be born again,
   Who would his Mother be?
"I," said Sorrow; and "I," said Pain;
   And "I," said Poverty.

But how, were Christ so made again,
   Could one be born of Three?
"Are not the griefs of earth a strain
   Of the Blessed Trinity?"

And who, on his birth-night, again
   His worshipers would be?
"Love," said Sorrow; and "Pity," said Pain;
   And "Peace," said Poverty.

And who the seers, from what strange lands,
   Would come to look at him?
"The simple and wise, with serving hands,
   And little ones light of limb."

And what would the kings of earth do then?
   "Put simple and wise to flight;
While loud in the darkened homes of men
   Little ones cried for light."

What use, what use, if once again
   The world rejects the Sign?
"Christ will still be a Lover of men,
   And his heart may be yours and mine.

"For this is the Tree whose blessed yield
   Bears seed in darkest ground;
And a wound by those bright leaves is healed,
   Wherever a wound is found."

                     EDWARD SHILLITO

## Never Night Again

The soft light from a stable door
  Lies on the midnight lands.
The Wise Men's star burns evermore
  Over all desert sands.

Unto all peoples of the earth
  A little Child brought light,
And never in the darkest place
  Can it be utter night.

No flickering torch, no wavering fire,
  But Light—the Life of men.
Whatever clouds may veil the sky,
  Never is night again!

LILIAN COX

## This Little Earth

Did He who wrought the universe
Of planet, star and moon
Not mold with special tenderness
This little earth, that soon
Should know an honor unsurpassed—
Should hold upon its sod,
Beside its quiet inland sea,
The Son of God?

LESLIE SAVAGE CLARK

### From "In Memoriam"

Tho' truths in manhood darkly join,
  Deep-seated in our mystic frame,
  We yield all blessing to the name
Of Him that made them current coin;

For Wisdom dealt with mortal powers,
  Where truth in closest words shall fail,
  When truth embodied in a tale
Shall enter in at lowly doors.

And so the Word had breath, and wrought
  With human hands the creed of creeds
  In loveliness of perfect deeds,
More strong than all poetic thought;

Which he may read that binds the sheaf,
  Or builds the house, or digs the grave,
  And those wild eyes that watch the wave
In roarings round the coral reef.

ALFRED TENNYSON

# In Nazareth

# In Nazareth

## From Nazareth

Comes any good from Nazareth?
  The scornful challenge as of old
Is flung on many a jeering breath
  From cloistered cells and marts of gold.

*What has Jesus of Nazareth got to say to us?*

Comes any good from Nazareth?
  Behold, the mighty Nazarene,
The Lord of life, the Lord of death,
  Through warring ages walks serene.

One touch upon his garment's fringe
  Still heals the hurt of bitter years.
Before him yet the demons cringe,
  He gives the wine of joy for tears.

39

O city of the Carpenter,
  Upon the hillslope old and gray,
The world amid its pain and stir
  Turns yearning eyes on thee today.

For he who dwelt in Nazareth,
  And wrought with toil of hand and brain,
Alone gives victory to faith
  Until the day he comes again.

MARGARET E. SANGSTER

## The Hidden Years

*to tune : "O Little Town of Bethlehem"*

The hidden years at Nazareth!
  How deep and still they seem,
Like rivers flowing in the dark
  Or waters in a dream!
Like waters under Syrian stars
  Reflecting lights above,
Repeating in their silent depths
  The wonder of God's love!

The hidden years at Nazareth!
  How clear and true they lie,
As open to the smile of God
  As to the Syrian sky!
As open to the heart of man
  As to the genial sun,
With dreams of vast adventuring,
  And deeds of kindness done!

The hidden years at Nazareth!
  How radiant they rise,
With life and death in balance laid
  Before a lad's clear eyes!
O Soul of Youth, forever choose,
  Forgetting fate or fear,
To live for truth or die with God,
  Who stands beside thee here!

ALLEN EASTMAN CROSS

## The Little Child

A simple-hearted Child was He,
  And He was nothing more;
In summer days, like you and me,
  He played about the door,
Or gathered, when the father toiled,
  The shavings from the floor.

Sometimes He lay upon the grass,
  The same as you and I,
And saw the hawks above Him pass
  Like specks against the sky;
Or, clinging to the gate, He watched
  The stranger passing by.

A simple Child, and yet, I think,
  The bird-folk must have known,
The sparrow and the bobolink,
  And claimed Him for their own,

And gathered round Him fearlessly
  When He was all alone.

The lark, the linnet, and the dove,
  The chaffinch and the wren,
They must have known His watchful love
  And given their worship then;
They must have known and glorified
  The Child who died for men.

And when the sun at break of day
  Crept in upon His hair,
I think it must have left a ray
  Of unseen glory there—
A kiss of love on that little brow
  For the thorns that it must wear.

             ALBERT BIGELOW PAINE

## Temple Offering

Did times grow hard in Nazareth
After Joseph went,
  Did hunger haunt that little home,
  Was Mary often spent
  With weariness?
  Perhaps remembering those years
  He, later, gauged aright
  The sacrificing love that marked
  A widow's mite.

             LESLIE SAVAGE CLARK

## A Legend

Christ, when a Child, a garden made,
  And many roses flourished there.
He watered them three times a day
  To make a garland for His hair.
And when in time the roses bloomed,
  He called the children in to share.
They tore the flowers from every stem
  And left the garden stript and bare.
"How wilt Thou weave Thyself a crown
  Now that Thy roses are all dead?"
"Ye have forgotten that the thorns
  Are left for Me," the Christ-child said.
They plaited then a crown of thorns
  And laid it rudely on His head;
A garland for His forehead made;
  For roses: drops of blood instead!
                    NATHAN HASKELL DOLE


## In Nazareth

During happy boyhood years
  He watched his mother go
About the house to bake, or wash
  The linen white as snow.

Later, he spoke of simple things,
 Of coin and lamp and broom,
Remembering belovèd days
 Within a humble room.
   LESLIE SAVAGE CLARK

## Hilltops

No doubt on the hills of Nazareth
 With many another lad
He scrambled, laughing, up the slopes,
 Flushed and young and glad.
How good that he knew love and mirth,
 However brief, until
The years when he must climb—alone—
 A last dark hill.
   LESLIE SAVAGE CLARK

## Young Jesus

"O little Son, upon your brow
 The blood runs red!
What hurt you so—comrades, perhaps?"
 "Thorns," he said.
   LESLIE SAVAGE CLARK

## The Carpenter

*X good on Ch. vocation*

Silent at Joseph's side he stood,
And smoothed and trimmed the shapeless wood.
And with firm hand, assured and slow,
Drove in each nail with measured blow.

Absorbed, he planned a wooden cask,
Nor asked for any greater task;
Content to make, with humble tools,
Tables and little children's stools.

Lord, give me careful hands to make
Such simple things as for Thy sake.
Happy within Thine House to dwell
If I may make one table well.

PHYLLIS HARTNOLL

## Young Man in a Galilean Doorway

Yes, utterly he loves his Nazareth:
The dusty village sprawling in the sun;
Rows of white houses harboring one by one
The hearts of plodding folk whom life and death
Receive as simply as their daily breath;
The dancing feet of children as they run
To meet him and entreat him share their fun;
Child eyes as wide as blue Gennesareth,

Deeper with wonder; fields of ripening grain;
New lilies; ox yokes smoothed of gall and pain;
The cool, clean workshop redolent of wood
And toil; the hill where dawn's first visions brood,
Beckoning to prayer like flags of hope unfurled:
He loves all that. And God so loves the world.

HERBERT D. GALLAUDET

## Crucifixion

He sang, too,
In the lanes of Nazareth,
With sunlit eyes, and boyish voice
Quickly out of breath.

He dreamed, too,
Of mountains and a city,
Where men would trample gems
And treasure pity.

He loved, too,
But someway friends forgot,
When swords and staves and kisses
Cut the lover's knot.

He grieved, too,
For all his songs unsung.
They gave him vinegar for songs
Upon a parching tongue.

He sighed, too,
With quickly failing breath,
For souls and songs and little lanes
In Nazareth.

EARL MARLATT

## Sight

In Nazareth he knew each narrow street,
The twisted paths that up the hillside crept,
The gleam of Galilee, where many a fleet
Of white-sailed vessels moved. He knew where swept
The terror of the ruthless Roman swords;
And, as he deftly planed his shining boards,
Of men, like books, he read the souls of them
Yet, "set his face toward Jerusalem."

Past the long, tortured road his spirit saw,
Further than broken lives, than ancient law,
Beyond the scourge, the cross, the bitter death,
His vision cast its flaming, living breath.

Two thousand years! And still we grope for light
Have mercy on us, Lord, and give us sight.

IDA NORTON MUNSON

## The Carpenter

Jesus was a carpenter. He gladly plied
His trade, for Nazareth had need of him.
Year after year he worked at Joseph's side:
He fashioned plows; set spokes to perfect rim;
Made seats of pine; smoothed bowls of cedarwood.
So tenderly he polished oxen yokes,
Men bared their hearts to him. He understood.
He helped each one. He loved the village folks,
Yet none of these could dream he was the Son
Of God! He was their brother, friend, who knew
The hidden good in each and, knowing, won
To strength. But Christ himself knew this was true:
He was the Father's Son in heart and mind,
The Light, the Way of Life, for all mankind.

Amy Bruner Almy

## The Carpenter of Nazareth

Were it table, trunk or stool
    Fashioned by his hand and tool,
The Carpenter of Nazareth
    Who Heaven and earth doth rule,

'Twere something just to view
    Handiwork he deigned to do;
'Twould shed on all our daily tasks
    A glory ever new.

For his work by ax or saw
  Would be all without a flaw,
Like his patience upon Calvary
  To magnify the Law.

Very dear the cross of shame
  Where he took the sinner's blame,
And the tomb wherein the Saviour lay,
  Until the third day came;

Yet he bore the selfsame load,
  And he went the same high road,
When the Carpenter of Nazareth
  Made common things for God.

WALTER SMITH

*Characteristic to Xst was the cross*

## Integrity

He made honest doors,
  Did Christ, the Nazarene;
He laid honest floors—
  His work was fine, and clean.

*good*

*Does integrity pay?*

He made crosses, too,
  Did Christ, the Crucified;
Straight and strong, and true—
  And on a cross he died.

WILLIAM L. STIDGER

## Carpenter

He sang at his bench in Nazareth
  While his strong young hands took hold
Of plank and nail to broaden the door
  For a shepherd neighbor's fold.

Into his hands on Calvary
  He took the nails again
To make the door which leads to God
  Wide for his fellow men.

                 LESLIE SAVAGE CLARK

## My Yoke Is Easy

The yokes he made were true.
Because the Man who dreamed
Was too
An artisan,
The burdens that the oxen drew
Were light.
At night
He lay upon his bed and knew
No beast of his stood chafing in a stall
Made restless by a needless gall.

The tenets of a man
May be full fine
But if he fails with plumb and line,

Scorns care,
Smooth planing,
And precision with the square,
Some neck will bear
The scar of blundering!

GLADYS LATCHAW

## When Spring Came to Nazareth

Sometimes the Man of Nazareth,
Bending above his awl and plane,
Must needs have paused with quickened breath
When spring brought respite from the rain,
And laid aside his tools to look
For birds beside some running brook.

Among the palms and fig-trees then,
Bright-jeweled by the heavy dew,
He must have walked rejoicing. When
The olives burst their buds, he knew.
He must have been, at summer's birth,
Glad in the raptures of the earth,

And, upon warm, sweet mornings, all
Unmindful of the awful hours
Of agony that would befall,
Gaining forgetfulness through flowers.
Surely, when petals filled the skies,
The Cross was hidden from his eyes.

MARY SINTON LEITCH

## Carpenter of Eternity

A carpenter, he worked with wood—
  The fragrant wood and pale:
He planed the broad and feathery coils
  And drove the drastic nail.

And from the cedar and the oak—
  The texture of the tree—
He built the House of Time before
  That of Eternity.

How strange to choose a carpenter
  And bind him and impale
Upon the wood he used to work—
  With the beloved nail!

E. MERRILL ROOT

## In the Carpenter Shop

I wish I had been his apprentice,
  To see him each morning at seven,
As he tossed his gray tunic about him,
  The Master of earth and of heaven;
When he lifted the lid of his work chest
  And opened his carpenter's kit,
And looked at his chisels and augers,
  And took the bright tools out of it;
When he gazed at the rising sun tinting
  The dew on the opening flowers,

And he smiled at the thought of his Father
  Whose love floods this fair world of ours;
When he fastened the apron about him,
  And put on his workingman's cap,
And grasped the smooth haft of his hammer
  To give the bent woodwork a tap,
Saying, "Lad, let us finish this ox yoke,
  The farmer must finish his crop."
Oh, I wish I had been his apprentice
  And worked in the Nazareth shop.

ANONYMOUS

*Business man's Christ*

## The Carpenter

I wonder what he charged for chairs at Nazareth
And did men try to beat him down
And boast about it in the town—
"I bought it cheap for half-a-crown
From that mad Carpenter"?

And did they promise and not pay,
Put it off to another day;
O, did they break his heart that way,
My Lord, the Carpenter?

I wonder did he have bad debts,
And did he know my fears and frets?
The gospel writer here forgets
To tell about the Carpenter.

*identified with us
here too ??*

But that's just what I want to know.
Ah! Christ in glory, here below
Men cheat and lie to one another so;
It's hard to be a carpenter.

G. A. STUDDERT-KENNEDY

## The Open Door

There passed the low door of the Nazareth home
"Men-of-the-earth," women with water jars,
The tinkling camel trains, soldiers of Rome,
And, in the quiet evening, when the stars
Shone over Galilee, shepherds, whose flocks
Grazed the high hills, moved slowly up the street
To take the night-watch, where gray, rugged rocks
Gave shade to pasture grasses, lush and sweet.

And One who watched the anxious world go by
Dreamed of a door unknown to human eye.

He saw its portal—fair, with peace alight;
Through hungry, troubled throngs the pathway led.
Sad faces lifted and dull eyes grew bright
When, "Follow me. . . . I am the door," he said.
Before he felt the scourge and climbed the hill
He knew man's spirit free forevermore;
In spite of death itself he visioned still
God's Kingdom through a lighted, open door.

And down the night, ignore it as men will,
They who bear crosses find it open still.

IDA NORTON MUNSON

## Irony of God

In vain
They shook their garments;
He did not hear the tinkling
Of little bells
On priestly hems;
Nor smell the smoky savor
Of slaughtered, burning life.

He did not see Jerusalem—
Nor Rome;
He passed by all "best families"
To dwell at last in Nazareth,
With Mary,
Mother of that Son
Who fraternized with fishermen;
Found heaven in little children;
And had a friend
Named Mary Magdalene.

EVA WARNER

## The Man of Galilee

He was no dreamer, dwelling in a cloud
   Of idle reason, strange philosophy;
In simple tasks his manhood strong he bowed
   Beneath hard toil and meager poverty.
Simple, not strange, the living words he saith—
The toiling Carpenter of Nazareth!

I cannot find him, when, with fertile brain
　I ponder strange amazing mystery;
But when my heart is darkened by the pain
　Of weariness or doubt or misery,
And someone smiles, or haply calls me friend,
　Or does a duty self-effacingly—
'Tis then his glowing face doth seem to bend
　Above me, and the living Christ I see—
The Son of God, the Man of Galilee!

HILDEGARDE HOYT SWIFT

*good*

### The Deathless Tale

Had he not breathed his breath
Truly at Nazareth;
Had not his very feet
Roamed many a hill and street;
Had Mary's story gone
To Time's oblivion;
Had the sweet record paled
And the truth not prevailed;
Dormant and bleak had been
This transitory scene,
And dark, thrice dark our earth
Unknowing of his birth.

The flowers beheld his face,
The stars knew his white grace.

The grass was greener for
His humble stable door;
The rose upon its stem
Redder for Bethlehem.
And we—are we not wise
To cling with avid eyes
To the old tale, and be
Moved by its memory?
Unutterably dim
Our bright world, lacking Him.

CHARLES HANSON TOWNE

## Jesus the Carpenter

If I could hold within my hand
  The hammer Jesus swung,
Not all the gold in all the land,
Nor jewels countless as the sand,
  All in the balance flung,
Could weigh the value of that thing
Round which his fingers once did cling.

If I could have the table Christ
  Once made in Nazareth,
Not all the pearls in all the sea,
Nor crowns of kings or kings to be
  As long as men have breath,
Could buy that thing of wood he made—
The Lord of Lords who learned a trade.

Yes, but his hammer still is shown
   By honest hands that toil,
And round his table men sit down;
And all are equals, with a crown
   Nor gold nor pearls can soil;
The shop of Nazareth was bare—
But brotherhood was builded there.

CHARLES M. SHELDON

*Here is true
Chr. Unionism.*

*"The Union of the Working Fellowship*

X

### Nazareth

Rome still holds her rod of power;
Paris charms an idle hour;
London, town of lords and kings,
Lures with stately traffickings;
But from all the earth we come,
Weary, spent, returning home!
Here we stand, with bated breath,
At the gates of Nazareth.

Little town, your sacred name
Bears no mark of warlike fame;
Kings and statesmen still despise
You and yours. The worldly wise
Give no thought to those strange tales—
That shall speak till living fails.
But we stand, with still, hushed breath
At the gates of Nazareth.

Once a lad, unknown and poor,
Standing at his humble door,
Had a dream of faith and hope.
Seeing men so blindly grope,
He would tell of God and good,
He envisioned brotherhood.
Thus we stand, with halting breath,
At the gates of Nazareth.

You, who dreamed of love and peace,
Prayed that warring soon might cease;
But today, 'mid wild alarms,
Nations rush again to arms.
But God's love illumed your dream;
Still abides its shining gleam
As we wait, with still, hushed breath
At the gates of Nazareth.

THOMAS CURTIS CLARK

# The Man Christ Jesus

# The Man Christ Jesus

## The Outdoor Son of God *Christ the Outdoorsman*

My Master was a man who knew
The rush of rain, the drip of dew;
The gentle kiss of midnight air
Upon his face upraised in prayer.

He was a man of lakes and stars;
He knew the Pleiades and Mars;
The silver of the Milky Way;
The night, the light, the dawn, the day.

His skin was bronzed like that of one
Who traveled under wind and sun;
His feet were stained by dusty ways;
His cheeks as brown as autumn days.

He walked alone upon the sea,
Spake peace to wave-washed Galilee;
All shores and seas were in his thought,
This man, God-bred, star-led, sky-taught.

He heard angelic, heavenly hymns
Sweep through the trembling leaves and limbs
Of Lebanon's old cedar trees;
Aeolian harps and harmonies.

To him there were no sweeter tones
Than water washing over stones;
To him no splendid symphony
Like murmuring, blue Galilee.

His hair was washed by summer showers;
He bent to kiss the wayside flowers;
Old Jordan's shore was sacred sod
To Christ, the outdoor Son of God!

William L. Stidger

### A Fisherman Speaks
#### (*Anno Domini 33*)

Oh, He who walked with fishermen
    Was man of men in Galilee;
He told us endless wonder-tales,
    His laugh was hale and free.

The water changed He into wine
   To please a poor man's company;
I saw Him walk one wretched night
   Upon a troubled sea.

And when the rabble cried for blood,
   I saw Him nailed upon a tree;
He showed how a brave man could die; )
   The Prince of men was He.

And rough men, we, who never wept,
   Wept when they nailed Him to the tree;
Oh, He was more than man, who walked
   With us in Galilee.

SCHARMEL IRIS

## He Worked

He worked! It is enough
That his own hands were
Tarnished with the stuff.
He knew the law's demands
For daily bread, the tasks,
The toils, the rude tools of his day;
The sweating face; nor did he ask,
In all his time, an easy way.

With hammer, saw and awkward wrench,
He proved himself the man.
Though Spirit-born, by the rude bench
He joined our race and ran

Its rugged course to where it ends.
While of a holier life he taught,
To which the soul ascends,
He lived, he wept, he wrought
With us—he called us friends.

J. N. Scholes

## Bread

He knew what hunger a man can feel,
  So he broke the fishes and bread
That the weary thousands who followed him
  Might be strengthened and fed.

He knew what hunger a soul can feel,
  Sharing the husks with swine,
So he gave his broken body and blood
  For bread and wine.

Leslie Savage Clark

## Jesus Was a Humble Man

Jesus was a humble man,
  Born in a carpenter's shack.
Planing boards and sawing boards
He made a cross
  To carry on his back.

Jesus went Golgotha's way
  To make all mankind free.

The cross he bore was yours
And mine—his death;
    He died for you and me.

Jesus was a humble man,
    Born in a carpenter's shack.
No one wants the cross he made
And no one has
    The heart to send it back.
                    RAYMOND KRESENSKY


## By the Sea of Galilee

Erect in youthful grace and radiant
    With spirit forces, all imparadised
In a divine compassion, down the slant
    Of these remembering hills he came, the Christ.
                    KATHARINE LEE BATES


## Comrade Christ

Give us Jesus Christ, the Carpenter.
What to us is your white-liveried God?
O men of the anvil, of the loom, the sod,
They have hid our God in a golden sepulcher;
They have made of our Christ a sniveling, pampered priest,
A paltry giver of fine bread and wine.
Our Christ is a God of men, as Man divine,
Holding in brotherhood the last and least.

He toils in the desert places by our side;
He delves with us beneath the granite hill;
He weeps above our brothers who have died;
He dreams with us in the darkness hot and still!
No surpliced shriver of the sins of men—
Christ, the Carpenter, has come again.

VERNE BRIGHT

## As He Walked With Us

Calm, strong and gentle Man of Galilee,
Whose heart by every human voice is stirred;
By whom are plaintive cries of creatures heard;
Whose eye escapes no tracery of tree,
Or modest wayside flower; alert to see
The fantasy of cloud, the flight of bird;
Whose ear can catch the faintest note and word
Of wind and stream, and distant western sea;
When I am treading on the open space,
Or threading slowly through the crowded marts,
Skilled Craftsman of the woods and market place,
Companion to all life and human hearts,
I crave, Thou unseen, understanding Guide,
To find Thee, silent, walking by my side.

HARRY WEBB FARRINGTON

## Beacon Light

Whenever I come on kelp-stained nets
  Drying along the sands,
I think of four bronzed fishermen,
  And my heart understands
How joyfully they laid aside
  Their nets by Galilee
To follow one clear Beacon Light
  Across eternity.

LESLIE SAVAGE CLARK

*good. The worker had a human feeling*

## Galilean

Sad searching eyes with benediction in their gaze,
  When other men's would flash the fire of hate,
Left not the lilies of the field unseen
  Nor left unseen the leper at the gate.

Strong hands that deftly shaped the oxen's bow,
  When other men's would scorn such lowly task,
Failed not to touch the eager blind man's eyes
  Nor ever failed to minister when asked.

Blest feet that walked the waves of Galilee
  Erstwhile in wilderness temptation spurned,
When other men's would take the valley road
  The pathless way up Calvary they turned.

MARGIELEA STONESTREET

## The Good Companion

Wayworn and weary,
  With feet stone-bruised and soiled,
He walked the dusty ways
  Of all the men who toiled.

Men who tilled the prairie
  And turned the teeming sod
Knew as they turned the furrow
  They walked and wrought with God.

The weary, heavy-laden,
  The humble toiling folk,
Knew who will lift the burden;
  He feels and shares their yoke.

The stony way he traveled
  Led to Calvary's stark hill,
But he walked with John and Peter,
  Knowing man's sorrows still.

The long, long way to Calvary
  His earthly footsteps led,
But John and Peter afterward
  Remembered what he said.

BELLE F. OWENS

## The World's Lone Lover

He was no stranger to salty tears, he
Who died upon a cedar tree;
He was a brother to ancient grief
And to the trembling olive leaf;
Or if you cross the distant bar *death*
He will be friendly as a star—
As a star, when men at sea,
Have lost the lights along the lea—
As a star when on some road
One man carries two men's load.
He is lover; he is friend;
And compensation at the journey's end.
He knows the alchemy of a tear;
He knows why we start and fear;
For he was flesh and knew why pain
Ceased for a day and came again;
He felt the flesh's blow and smart,
Caught life's arrow in his heart,
But smiled—smiled and then forgave—
There is no darkness in his grave.

                          J. R. PERKINS

## The Splendid Lover

One and one only is the splendid Lover,
   The all-forgiving, all-compassionate;
When others fret you with impatient loving,
   He a greater Lover patiently will wait.
Though you turn from him threescore times and seven,
   Mock his devotion, spurn him as a guest,
With steadfast wooing, he at last will win you,
   And reveal life's wonder when your head lies on his
     breast.

JOHN RICHARD MORELAND

*[handwritten marginalia: "true", "X", "He loves us when we spurn Him"]*

## Alone Into the Mountain

All day from that deep well of life within
Himself has He drawn healing for the press
Of folk, restoring strength, forgiving sin,
Quieting frenzy, comforting distress.
Shadows of evening fall, yet wildly still
They throng Him, touch Him, clutch His garment's hem,
Fall down and clasp His feet, cry on Him, till
The Master, spent, slips from the midst of them
And climbs the mountain for a cup of peace,
Taking a sheer and rugged track untrod
Save by a poor lost sheep with thorn-torn fleece
That follows on and hears Him talk with God.

KATHARINE LEE BATES

## Tempted *Lk 4*

Into the wilderness
Straightway our Lord was driven of the Spirit;
Swept by that stress
Of rapture, sun and stars were but one shining
Till forty days had passed
And, Son of Man though Son of God, he hungered.

Why should he fast
With power to make stones bread; why fear, with succor
Of angels at his call;
Why fail, when all the world was to his Father
A golden ball,
One out of many, but a little present
For a belovèd Son?
*Joy*
Ecstasy, faint with its own bliss, encountered *Heb 12²*
The scorpion
Of self, love's enemy. For love is holy
In loving; love is safe
Only in saving; love, despised, rejected, *love*
The world's white waif,
Needs nothing that this earth can give of glory,
For love dwelleth in God.
*deity*                                    *humanity*   *Person of Christ*
So Christ's immortal rose above his mortal
And on it trod.

KATHARINE LEE BATES

### The Wilderness

*Good description of the mountain of temptation* ✓

Up from the Jordan straight his way he took
To that lone wilderness, where rocks are hurled,
And strewn, and piled—as if the ancient world
In strong convulsions seethed and writhed and shook,
Which heaved the valleys up, and sunk each brook,
And flung the molten rock like ribbons curled
In midst of gray around the mountains whirled:—
A grim land, of a fierce, forbidding look.
The wild beasts haunt its barren stony heights,
And wilder visions came to tempt him there;
For forty days and forty weary nights,
Alone he faced his mortal self and sin, ?
Chaos without, and chaos reigned within,
Subdued and conquered by the might of prayer.

CAROLINE HAZARD

### Temptation

*excellent*

They took him to a mountain top to see
Where earth's fair kingdoms flung their golden net
To snare the feet and trick the souls of men.
With slimy craft and cynic guile they said:—
If he but sees the glory and the pride,
The pomps and pleasures of this tinsel world,
He will forget his splendid futile dreams.
And so they took him up and tempted him.

They pointed far across their level earth,
East to the fabled empires of the Ind,
Whose rulers' power was as the power of gods,
Where caravans with tinkling camel-bells
Brought silks and perfumes, pearls and ivory,
And tribute from far humbled provinces;
South to the magic kingdom of the Nile,
To Nubia and Abyssinia,
Jungle and desert kingdoms, rude but rich
With slaves and gems and golden yellow sands;
Northward to barbarous lands but dimly seen,
Savage but surging with unmeasured strength; *cf. nationalism*
West where Rome's empire sent her legions forth,
Conquering, building, ruling with wise force,
The mighty mother of an unborn brood
Of nations which should rise and rule the world.

All this they spread before him, tempting him,
And watched to see ambition light his eye,
The lust of power darken his bright face,
And avarice crook his hands to clutch the gold.

But from the mountain peak he raised his eyes,
And saw the deep, calm sky, the stars, and God.

WINFRED ERNEST GARRISON

## Vision

It is a thread—a tiny, shining thread—
That weaves its way in home, in shop and street;
It skirts the busy paths that know the tread
Of young and dancing, old and tired feet.
Men glimpse its light but dimly, now and then,
As though it beckoned where some lofty track
Leads upward to a dream that might have been—
Above life's deep discouragement and lack.

But One there was who knew the commonplace
Touched with its glory, simple, yet divine.
He saw the yearning soul in every face,
And sensed the dignity of life's design.
Yet, men still dread his vision to embrace—
So poor the upper room, the bread and wine.

IDA NORTON MUNSON

*lovely.*

## One There Was

One there was who, passing by,
Touched all life with alchemy;
Grass of field or birds of air
Made his heart of God aware.
Of common salt or smooth-worn yoke
A figure patterned for eager folk;
Of wayside spring or granary
Symbols he made which never die;

*Nature aglow with God totten*

*Took the comon thiengs a sacramental word.*

*ables*

From mustard seed or branching vine,
Similitudes of things divine.
Meaning to leavening dough he lent;
He made, of bread, a sacrament.

STELLA FISHER BURGESS

## Son of Man

He often spoke of things of home,
   Of linen white as snow,
Of platters cleansed inside and out,
   Of leaven hid in dough,
And lost coin sought with broom and lamp.
   Was he wistful, he
Who walked, alone, the road toward death,
   Homeless in Galilee?

LESLIE SAVAGE CLARK

## Contrast *Jn. 6 Adulterous woman*

What wrote he on the parched and dusty ground
When men brought to him one condemned in sin
Whose life an ugly, tangled web had been?
The sneering mob stalked haughtily around
And mocked the woman, while the clamorous sound
Of raucous voices grew into a din
That shrieked and cursed at her and all her kin,
As she in silence stood, with terror bound.

They faced each other—he the Stainless One,
And she the harlot—vilely sick within.
The brutes who brought her, by his will outdone,
Each one, himself, perchance, a libertine,
Slunk off, and left them standing there alone,
And, at his word, she rose up, white and clean.

*beautiful*

AUBERT EDGAR BRUCE

## To Him All Life Was Beauty

To him all life was Beauty. The sun upon the hills,
The sweeping shadows, and the winding lane.
Morning he loved, with dewdrops on the flowers;
Evening, with sunset and soft, warm April rain.
Friends he found in lepers stumbling to him,
Love in those who hate, grace in sinners' eyes.
Dawn he saw with all earth's new-born glory,
Twilight and darkness, and hope in human sighs.
Youth was his, and springtime, and music in the trees;
Life was his, and sunshine, and the murmuring of the bees;
Joy in healing broken hearts; manhood's noble strife;
All the wonder and the beauty of a sacred human life.

He walked the common lanes, the city streets he trod,
And in his heart was Beauty . . . the Beauty born of God.

A. L. C.

## He, Too, Loved Beauty

I who love beauty in the open valleys,
  Tintings of sunset, and the swallow's flight,
Must breathe the air of squalid city alleys,
  Shut from the cool caresses of the night.
Wistful of fragrance where the springtime dallies,
  Sharing with sordid souls a city's blight.

He, too, loved beauty, but a city drew him.
  Flowers he found in little children's eyes;
Something of grace in lepers stumbling to him;
  Fragrance from spikenard split in sweet surprise;
Joy in forgiving men at last who slew him;
  Courage in service, hope in sacrifice.

                    EDWIN McNEILL POTEAT

## The Poet of Palestine

Poet, Jesus, speak to me,
Poet of the hill and sea,
Singing by blue Galilee.

Poet, Jesus, you who knew
When the sky was deep and blue,
Mirrored in a drop of dew.

Poet, Jesus, laughing seer,
You who brought the stars so near,
You who made a child so dear.

You who knew the deep distress
Of a lone adventuress;          *Jn 6 -*
Knew to love, forgive, and bless.

Poet, Jesus, would I too
Were as tender, and as true,          *yes!*
With all outcasts as were you!

You who knew the stalk and seed
Of each lovely flower and weed,
Of each dream, and hope, and deed.

Poet, Jesus, you who saw
Something like eternal law;
Love, redeeming every flaw.

Poet, Jesus of the sea
Men now know as Galilee,
And a hill called Calvary;

Poet of the tree and sod,
Poet of the sky and clod
Pointing to the stars of God.

Poet, Jesus, Shepherd, King,
Teach me how to laugh and sing
Over every simple thing!

WILLIAM L. STIDGER

## To the Master Poet

They do you wrong who paint you, wondrous Man,
A pale ascetic, worn with argument
Of God and man, of life, of death, of sin;
A pilgrim here, with thoughts on other spheres.
They do you wrong: for you had eyes and ears
For this our lovely earth, its trees and flowers,
Its fields of corn, its choirs of happy birds;
You thrilled at dawn, rejoiced when spring began.
Thus were you Poet. Too, you had your dreams:
That John and Peter, James and Magdalene,
Dark Judas too, should learn to know your God.
You had the faith to hail the Kingdom's gleams
In earth's embattled realm; and still your hope
Is undismayed, though men in darkness grope.

THOMAS CURTIS CLARK

## Mary

With love that counted not the cost,
    She broke the alabaster; filled
With but one thought: It was her Friend
    For whom the precious gift was spilled.

THOMAS CURTIS CLARK

### Christ's Giving

The spirit of self-sacrifice
Stays not to count the price.

Christ did not of his mere abundance cast
Into the empty treasury of man's store:
   The First and Last
Gave until even he could give no more;
   His very living,
   Such was Christ's giving.
            ANNA E. HAMILTON

### Ave Maria Gratia Plena

*The humbleness of Jesus' birth*

Was this His coming! I had hoped to see
A scene of wondrous glory, as was told
Of some great God who in a rain of gold
Broke open bars and fell on Danae:
Or a dread vision as when Semele
Sickening for love and unappeased desire
Prayed to see God's clear body, and the fire
Caught her brown limbs and slew her utterly:
With such glad dreams I sought this holy place,
And now with wondering eyes and heart I stand
Before this supreme mystery of Love:
Some kneeling girl with passionless pale face,
An angel with a lily in his hand,
And over both the white wings of a Dove.
            OSCAR WILDE

*Jesus would not support our war-machine*

## Hands of Christ

Hands of Christ,
Divine hands of a carpenter. . . .
I cannot imagine those hands
Forging lances, anviling swords,
Or designing a new model of bomber;
Those hands, hands of Christ,
Were the hands of a carpenter.

Hands of Christ, calloused
Carving cradles,
Shaping plows, building life. . . .
I cannot imagine those hands
Busied with cannon,
Explosive and grenades;
Those calloused hands
Became calloused building life. *hot deal*

Among the feverish hands
That build cruisers
And bombers,
His hands are not found!
His bear the marks of nails,
Heroic marks of sacrifice;
Those hands, bleeding hands,
Strong, steel-nerved hands,
Are the vigorous hands of a carpenter
Quietly building life.

FRANCISCO E. ESTRELLO
*(Translated by H. M. Sein)*

## The Hands of Christ

A Baby's hands in Bethlehem
  Were small and softly curled,
But held within their dimpled grasp
  The hope of half a world.

A Carpenter's in Nazareth
  Were skilled with tool and wood;
They laid the beams of humble homes
  And found their labor good.

A Healer's hands in Galilee
  Were stretched toward all who came
For Him to cleanse their hidden wounds
  Or cure the blind and lame.

Long, long ago the hands of Christ
  Were nailed upon a tree,
But still their holy touch redeems
  The hearts of you and me.
                    LESLIE SAVAGE CLARK


## My Master's Face

No pictured likeness of my Lord have I;
He carved no record of his ministry
          On wood or stone.
He left no sculptured tomb nor parchment dim,
But trusted for all memory of him
          Men's hearts alone.

Who sees the face but sees in part; who reads
The spirit which it hides, sees all; he needs
    No more. Thy grace—
Thy life in my life, Lord, give Thou to me;
And then, in truth, I may forever see
    My Master's face!
WILLIAM HURD HILMER

*[handwritten margin note: The Spirit best reveals Christ]*

## Comrade Jesus

I tramped the pavement, blaming God,
When there beside me Jesus trod.

Now we shall walk, this Friend and I,
Across the earth, the sea, the sky. *[handwritten: dealt]*

I do not know what he may be; *[handwritten: doctrinally]*
I only know he walks with me.

From Eden barred and Paradise,
Too wisely sad, too sadly wise!

Oh, lonely feet! Oh, bleeding feet
In step with mine on city street!
RALPH CHEYNEY

## Afternoon in a Church

*[handwritten margin note: church is a workday]*

I have grown tired of routine work
    And I have come to whisper a Name.
O, let men laugh and say I shirk,
    Beaten in the money game.

*[handwritten margin note: worship on Sunday]*

I hear a step; One comes to me
   And places his hand upon my head.
I feel the touch and I can see
   The finger tips are red.

His touch relieves the throbbing ache.
   He washes my tired and burning feet;
For he has been where crosses break,
   And comes here from the street.

RAYMOND KRESENSKY


## Christ and We

Christ took our nature on him not that he
'Bove all things loved it, for the purity:
No, but he dressed him with our human trim,
Because our flesh stood most in need of him.

ROBERT HERRICK


## From "The Ring and the Book"

I never realized God's birth before,
How he grew likest God in being born.

  .    .    .    .    .    .

Such ever was love's way—to rise, it stoops.

ROBERT BROWNING

## We Would See Jesus

We would see Jesus! We would look upon
The light in that divinely human face,
Where lofty majesty and tender grace
  In blended beauty shone.

We would see Jesus, and would hear again
The voice that charmed the thousands by the sea,
Spoke peace to sinners, set the captives free,
  And eased the sufferers' pain.

We would see Jesus, yet not him alone—
But see ourselves as in our Maker's plan;
And in the beauty of the Son of Man
  See man upon his throne.

We would see Jesus, and let him impart
The truth he came among us to reveal,
Till in the gracious message we should feel
  The beating of God's heart.

                        W. J. SUCKOW

## The Kingdom

"Where is the Kingdom?" asked the pompous priest,
Weighted with lore, and spent with fast and feast.
The lowly Christ on his pretensions smiled,
And simply said, "In the heart of a little child."

                        THOMAS CURTIS CLARK

### Blind Bartimeus

Blind Bartimeus at the gates
Of Jericho in darkness waits;
He hears the crowd—he hears a breath
Say, "It is Christ of Nazareth!"
And calls, in tones of agony,
"Jesus, have mercy now on me!"

The thronging multitudes increase;
Blind Bartimeus, hold thy peace!
But still, above the noisy crowd,
The beggar's cry is shrill and loud;
Until they say, "He calleth thee!"
"Fear not, arise, He calleth thee!"

Then saith the Christ, as silent stands
The crowd, "What wilt thou at my hands?"
And he replies, "O give me light!
Rabbi, restore the blind man's sight!"
And Jesus answers, "Go in peace,
Thy faith from blindness gives release!"

Ye that have eyes, yet cannot see,
In darkness and in misery,
Recall those mighty Voices Three,
"Jesus, have mercy now on me!
Fear not, arise, and go in peace!
Thy faith from blindness gives release!"

HENRY WADSWORTH LONGFELLOW

### The Teacher

He sent men out to preach the living Word,
  Aflame with all the ardor of his fire;
They spoke the Truth wherever truth was heard,
  But back to him they brought their hearts' desire;
They turned to him through all the lengthening days
  With each perplexity of life or creed.
His deep reward, not that they spoke his praise,
  But that they brought to him their human need.

HILDEGARDE HOYT SWIFT

### The Man Christ

He built no temple, yet the farthest sea
Can yield no shore that's barren of His place
  For bended knee.

He wrote no book, and yet His words and prayer
Are intimate on many myriad tongues,
  Are counsel everywhere.

The life He lived has never been assailed,
Nor any precept, as He lived it, yet
  Has ever failed.

He built no kingdom, yet a King from youth
He reigned, is reigning yet; they call His realm
  The kingdom of the Truth.

THERESE LINDSEY

# The Way of the Cross

# The Way of the Cross

### Palm Sunday and Monday

They pluck their palm branches and hail him as King,
    Early on Sunday;
They spread out their garments; hosannas they sing,
    Early on Sunday.

But where is the noise of their hurrying feet,
    The crown they would offer, the scepter, the seat?
Their King wanders hungry, forgot in the street,
    Early on Monday.

EDWIN McNEILL POTEAT

*Jesus's burrow speaks*

## Riding Through Jerusalem

I thought it strange he asked for me,
  And bade me carry him,
The noblest one of all the earth,
  Into Jerusalem!

But rumor goes he loved the meek
  And such on him might call,
That may be why he trusted me
  The humblest beast of all.

Yet though he was so great and wise
  Unequaled in his might,
I scarcely knew I bore a King,
  So light he rode—so light!

They sang Hosannah in the streets,
  But I have heard men say
The only time they praised their King
  Was when he rode that day.

Men pushed and shouted all around,
  The air was thick with cries,
They spread their garments at my feet,
  And palms before mine eyes.

They strewed the narrow road with boughs
  And barred my path again—
But the tenderest hand I ever felt
  Was on my bridle chain.

                    MARION SUSAN CAMPBELL

*The righteous man regardeth the life of the beast.*

### Wednesday in Holy Week

Man's life is death. Yet Christ endured to live
  Preaching and teaching, toiling to and fro,
Few men accepting what he yearned to give,
  Few men with eyes to know
  His face, that Face of Love he stooped to show.

Man's death is life. For Christ endured to die
  In slow unuttered weariness of pain,
A curse and an astonishment, passed by,
  Pointed at, mocked again
  By men for whom he shed his blood—in vain?
                                    CHRISTINA G. ROSSETTI

### Holy Week

"And having taken bread, he broke it,"
(Weary men within a dimly lighted room);
"He blessed it saying, 'This is my body, eat,'"
(Three crosses faintly outlined in the night);
"This cup contains a hallowed drink, my blood,"
(Lilies at dawn, before the empty tomb);
"Preserve thy soul to everlasting life,"
(A dark church, altar candles' flickering light);
"Arise, let us go hence."

Far out upon a lonely hill tonight,
Against dark oaks, a wild plum blossoms white.
                                    PHOEBE SMITH BACHELDER

*(margin note, left: "excellent")*

## With Me in Paradise

If I had sat at supper with the Lord
And laid my head upon that saving breast,
I might have turned and fled among the rest—
I might have been that one who left the board
To add the high priest's silver to his hoard.
Had our Redeemer stooped to wash my feet,
Would I have washed my neighbor's, clean and sweet,
Or thrice denied the Christ I had adored?

Long have I grieved that I was not Saint Paul
Who rode those seas and saw the tempest toss
The ships he sailed in when he heard the call
To preach the risen Christ and gain through loss.

Tonight I envy most among them all
That thief who hung repentant on his cross.

ALEXANDER HARVEY

*(margin note, left, handwritten: "We are sinful, unpardonable / Oh to have the grace is in every hour / to be penitent")*

## This Is My Body

He saw the Word that spake it,
He took the bread and brake it;
And what that Word did make it,
I do believe and take it.

JOHN DONNE

*(margin note, left, handwritten: "Eucharist")*

## The Upper Room

Oh, had it been mine, that upper room,
To make all fair with oil and bloom!
I'd spread clean rushes on the floor,
Put water jug and towel by the door;
A linen cloth as white as May,
A runner, on the table lay.
I have no incense, only bread and wine;
The grapes and winepress, they are mine;
My bread, as spikenard redolent,
Is of all wholesome odors blent.
Then, having made all fresh and fair,
I would give thanks for this my share.

BELLE F. OWENS

## Two Chalices

There was a chalice in the ancient East
Unhallowed by the Master of the Feast;
It did not catch the sacramental tide
That welled from Jesus' lacerated side,
Nor lure Sir Galahad to seek the shrine
Whence glowed its radiance and flowed its wine.
It was abandoned at a village well
When once a passing stranger stopped to tell
Of founts of living water that may spring
Within the soul, and make the spirit sing.

Two sacred chalices I shall acclaim:
One from an upper room; of lesser fame
One from a well, illumined by his name.

EDWIN McNEILL POTEAT

## Communion

Not to the twelve alone
Within that upper room,
Not only to the waiting throngs
Who kneel in Thy cathedrals
Hast Thou ordained
The sacrament of food and drink;
Whoso has bowed his head—
Invoking Thy love—
And shared a frugal fare
With brother, beggar, friend,
Has eaten holy bread.

Whoso has eaten to excess,
Or drunk the drink of gluttony,
Has forfeited the Body to decay,
Has spilt the Blood.

PHOEBE SMITH BACHELDER

## Remembrance

The sun lay warm on tawny fields
  Of wheat in Galilee,
Where lilies swayed and winds were soft
  Beside a summer sea.

There purple vineyards climbed the slopes
  And fragrance filled the air,
While flocks of doves on silver wings
  Ascended like a prayer.

Was he, perhaps, remembering
  The peace of wheat and vine
That night he made a sacrament
  Of bread and wine?

LESLIE SAVAGE CLARK

## Judas

"And one that dips with me the sop."—"Not I!"
  He rises from the quiet group he knew
Before the priestly court: "What will you buy?"
  For thirty pieces he bought death for two. — *He who betrays Christ, takes his own life too.*

HOWARD MCKINLEY CORNING

### Judas Iscariot

*On Judas talking to hisself*

Judas was I! Ah, the mockery!
  For I thought he could not die.
What did the silver mean to me
  When I heard my Master's cry?

If I had known that he understood;
  Forgave me! Aye, and blessed!
Would I have taken the coward's way
  If I had known or guessed?

Greater my grief than heart could bear
  After the fear and doubt;
What was left in the world for me
  After the Light was out?

Margaret Nickerson Martin

### Values

*On love of money*

How strange and pitiful that man
Through centuries has clung
To coins for wealth, and can forget
The thirty pieces flung
Aside in wild remorse, . . . forget
A tree where Judas hung!

Leslie Savage Clark

## "The Lord Turned, and Looked Upon Peter"

The Saviour looked on Peter. Aye, no word,
No gesture of reproach! the heavens serene,
Though heavy with armed justice, did not lean
Their thunders that way! the forsaken Lord
Looked only on the traitor. None record
What that look was, none guess: for those who have seen
Wronged lovers loving through a death-pang keen,
Or pale-cheeked martyrs smiling to a sword,
Have missed Jehovah at the judgment-call.
And Peter, from the height of blasphemy—
"I never knew this man"—did quail and fall,
As knowing straight that God—and turned free
And went out speechless from the face of all,
And filled the silence, weeping bitterly.

ELIZABETH BARRETT BROWNING

## The Meaning of the Look

I think that look of Christ might seem to say—
"Thou Peter! art thou then a common stone
Which I at last must break my heart upon,
For all God's charge to His high angels may
Guard my foot better? Did I yesterday
Wash thy feet, my beloved, that they should run
Quick to deny me 'neath the morning sun?
And do thy kisses, like the rest, betray?

The cock crows coldly.—Go, and manifest
A late contrition, but no bootless fear!
For when thy final need is dreariest,
Thou shalt not be denied, as I am here;
My voice to God and angels shall attest,
*Because I know this man, let him be clear.*"

ELIZABETH BARRETT BROWNING

## The Focus of That Face

Peter denied, but Jesus did not scold.
He knew the loneliness, the numbing cold,
The leering jest, the cruel taunting word—
Peter denied him once, and Jesus heard.

Peter denied, but Jesus did not cry
A protest at the oath, or at the lie.
The winds of desolation blew and blew—
Peter denied him twice, and Jesus knew.

Thrice he denied; then Jesus broke the trance
With one determined, reassuring glance;
And love was won from terror's dark embrace
Beneath the radiant focus of that Face.

EDWIN MCNEILL POTEAT

## The Crowd

Always He feared you;
For you knew Him only as the man of loaves and fishes—
The man who did marvelous things.
He who raised Lazarus,
Healed the lame, and made the blind to see,
Fleeing from you, He sought the solace of the garden.

He must have known
That you would cry, "Release unto us Barabbas!"
And fling your cruel words at Him
As He climbed to Golgotha alone.
Perhaps He knew
That some day you would build creeds about Him,
And lose Him in massive structures of stone,
With costly windows, dignified ritual, and eloquent
    preachers;
While outside He waited . . .
Sad . . . and alone.

IRENE McKEIGHAN

## Judgment

They hailed him, trembling, to the Judgment Seat.
"O Lord, the man who made the nails that pierced Thy
        feet!"
The Master laid a thin, scarred hand upon the shame-
        bowed head.
"They were good nails," he said.

KENNETH W. PORTER

## Before Pilate

What utter loneliness he knew
    When his own race could plot
His death, when those he healed had fled,
    Their benefits forgot—
And, thrice, a loved disciple vowed,
    "I know him not!"

LESLIE SAVAGE CLARK

## The Lonely Christ

The many now had left him, melting fast
    As trembling courtiers from a fallen king;
But were there none beside him at the last
    To whom his love could cling?

Twelve men that night were left; he ate with them
  And pledged the Victor's feast; then led the way
Through moonlit alleys of Jerusalem
  Across the brook to pray.

One he had lost; the others wearied slept;
  With no man by his side the Lord fought on.
They fled into the night; and he was swept
  From court to court alone.

Through solitary ways to peopled lands;
  By desert paths into a city throng;
Silent he went alone, that pilgrim bands
  Might follow him with song.

EDWARD SHILLITO

## His Passion

*lovely*

A heap of stones lay at his command,
Stones hurled at him
By cruel hands.
Some bruised him deeply,
Yet none were hurled
In return.
Instead, there is an altar there—
That heap of stones.

GEORGE CONRAD PULLMAN

*classic*

## A Ballad of Trees and the Master

Into the woods my Master went,
   Clean forspent, forspent.
Into the woods my Master came,
   Forspent with love and shame.
But the olives they were not blind to Him,
The little gray leaves were kind to Him:
The thorn-tree had a mind to Him
   When into the woods He came.

Out of the woods my Master went,
   And He was well content.
Out of the woods my Master came,
   Content with death and shame.
When Death and Shame would woo Him last,
From under the trees they drew Him last:
'Twas on a tree they slew Him—last
   When out of the woods He came.

SIDNEY LANIER

## Resignation

He prayed by the stone
Where they left him all alone;
And he watched for the light
Of the torches through the night.

He bowed his head and wept
While the three disciples slept
Where he watched for the light
Of the torches through the night.

And there came the gift of calm
Like some heavenly peace and balm
As he watched for the light
Of the torches through the night.

Then a surge of strength and power
Came to him that tragic hour
Where he watched for the light
Of the torches through the night.

WILLIAM L. STIDGER

## Malchus
(*Servant of the High Priest*)   X Malchus talks

We crossed Brook Cedron to Gethsemane.
I had not seen his face nor heard his voice;
To seek him there and bind him was for me
A mandate questioned not. I knew no choice.
My arm held high a torch to better know
The one whom Judas kissed. And then a blow
Burned from a flashing blade. All thoughts grew dim.
My head dripped blood. I had forgotten him—
Until I felt a touch that cooled and healed.

His look of tenderness! Was that what stirred
The soul of me? My heart and nerve were steeled
To cruel deeds. And yet, his words I heard
Stayed with me—patient, kind, as spoke the Lord:
"I am the one ye seek . . . put up thy sword."

IDA NORTON MUNSON

## Go to Dark Gethsemane

Go to dark Gethsemane,
 Ye that feel the tempter's power;
Your Redeemer's conflict see;
 Watch with Him one bitter hour;
Turn not from His griefs away;
Learn of Jesus Christ to pray.

Follow to the judgment-hall,
 View the Lord of life arraigned;
O the wormwood and the gall!
 O the pangs His soul sustained!
Shun not suffering, shame or loss;
Learn of Him to bear the cross.

Calvary's mournful mountain climb;
 There adoring at His feet,
Mark that miracle of time,
 God's own sacrifice complete;
"It is finished!" hear the cry;
Learn of Jesus Christ to die.

JAMES MONTGOMERY

## The Dissenter

Before the altar in his heart he knelt
And offered up his soul's long agony;
Forgiveness sought, and wrestled with his God—
Conscious, in losing, of eternal gain.

No outward symbols fed his soul's deep need,
No tonsured priest between himself and God,
No swinging censers lulled his sense of sin,
But through the bare, high windows the white light
Softly across his humbled shoulders cast
The shadow of the cross.

LILLIAN M. SWENSON

## From Bethlehem to Calvary

From Bethlehem to Calvary the Saviour's journey lay;
Doubt, unbelief, scorn, fear and hate beset him day by day,
But in his heart he bore God's love that brightened all
the way.

O'er the Judean hills he walked, serene and brave of soul,
Seeking the beaten paths of men, touching and making
whole,
Dying at last for love of man, on Calvary's darkened
knoll.

He went with patient step and slow, as one who scatters
　　seed;
Like a fierce hunger in his heart he felt the world's great
　　need,
And the negations Moses gave he changed to loving deed.

From Bethlehem to Calvary the world still follows on,
Even as the halt and blind of old along his path were
　　drawn;
Through Calvary's clouds they seek the light that led him
　　to the dawn.

MEREDITH NICHOLSON

*— here we find meaning*

## The Blessed Road

*good*

Three roads led out to Calvary;
　　The first was broad and straight,
That Pilate and great Caiaphas
　　Might ride thereon in state.

The second was the felon's road,
　　Cruel and hard to tread
For those who bore the cross's load,
　　For those whose footsteps bled.

The third road slunk through mean defiles,
　　Fearing the open sky;
And Judas crept the dreadful miles
　　To Calvary thereby.

The highroad up to Calvary
    Was blotted from the land;
Where Judas hid, the jackal cries
    By thorn-cursed drifts of sand.

But that poor road the felons went—
    How fair it now appears,
Smoothed wide by myriads penitent
    And flower-set by their tears!

CHARLES BUXTON GOING

### Simon of Cyrene

I walked that day out to the death-marked hill—
They call the place "the skull"—and saw him bear
His cross until he fell. It was not fair,
I thought, to place it on him. Strength and skill
Were mine from country toil. I bore it till
We came to Golgotha. I did not dare
To speak my grief; I only thought to spare
Him pain—his grateful look lives with me still.

And as we walked along, some women wept.
I could not censure them—my eyes were dim.
But know ye what he said? His words I've kept
Within my heart these years for love of him:
"Weep not for me. Dark days await you too.
Forgive these men: they know not what they do."

GEORGIA HARKNESS

*on the race question*

## Simon the Cyrenian Speaks

Look not on me with scorn because
  My skin's of darker hue—
Remember once these shoulders bore
  The cross he bore for you.

                  GLEN BAKER

## Men Follow Simon

They spat in his face and hewed him a cross
On that dark day.
The cross was heavy; Simon bore it
Golgotha way.
  O Master, the cross is heavy!

They ripped his hands with driven nails
And flayed him with whips.
They pressed the sponge of vinegar
To his parched lips.
  O Master, Thy dear blood drips!

Men follow Simon, three and three,
And one and one,
Down through valleys and up long hills
Into the sun.
  O Master, Master—into the sun!

                  RAYMOND KRESENSKY

### Good Friday

"The Son of God am I," he humbly said,
 And yet his torturers believed him not.
They taunted, scourged, and spat upon their Lord,
 And took possession of his clothes by lot.

They crucified him—watched him as he died;
 And long before his blood dried on the sod,
When nature turbulently voiced its ire,
 They fearfully admitted: He is God.

ALICE B. JURICA

### Calvary

Friendless and faint, with martyred steps and slow,
Faint for the flesh, but for the spirit free,
Stung by the mob that came to see the show,
The Master toiled along to Calvary;
We gibed him, as he went, with houndish glee,
Till his dim eyes for us did overflow;
We cursed his vengeless hands thrice wretchedly,
And this was nineteen hundred years ago.

But after nineteen hundred years the shame
Still clings, and we have not made good the loss
That outraged faith has entered in his name.
Ah, when shall come love's courage to be strong!
Tell me, O Lord—tell me, O Lord, how long
Are we to keep Christ writhing on the cross!

EDWIN ARLINGTON ROBINSON

## Recognition

When Christ went up to Calvary,
   His crown upon His head,
Each tree unto its fellow-tree
   In awful silence said:
"Behold the Gardener is He
   Of Eden and Gethsemane!"
           JOHN BANISTER TABB

## Resurgam

It happened on an April day,
Bounded by skies so blue and still,
A Man was led a cruel way,
Cross-laden, towards a skull-shaped hill,
Followed by a mob whose piercing cry
Was, "Crucify!"

It happened on an April morn,
A Man was nailed upon a tree
Whose head was circled with sharp thorn,
And lifted high that all might see
His agony of failing breath,
His awful death.

It happened on an April eve . . .
The air was cut by one sharp cry
That wine or gall could not relieve:

"*Eli . . . lama . . . sabacthani . . .*"
Then lightning, thunder, crack on crack,
The sun went black.

It happened on an April day . . .
They tombed a Man with seals of lead,
Set guards to watch, who would gainsay
His words and show that he was dead,
Proving himself he could not save
From the dark grave.

> JOHN RICHARD MORELAND

## Contrast

And it was in the winter
  When all the world was bare
That God came down to Bethlehem
  And found a shelter there.

But it was in the springtime
  When all was bright and fair
They took our God to Calvary
  And let him suffer there.

> CHARLES GRANVILLE HAMILTON

## One April Day

Who could be sad in April
  When spring's green surging sea
Is breaking into crested waves
  On every flowering tree?

The lonely waiting seed
  Throws off a seamless coat,
And mirthful songs are trembling
  In every lyric throat.

I know one April day,
  In agony, Christ died;—
But on an April day he, too,
  Was glorified.

JOHN RICHARD MORELAND

## Two Crosses

A fiery cross against the night,
  Men fleeing, terror-blind—
(The Cross I know means gentleness
  Toward all of humankind).

A cross that seeks to purge with flame
  The evil from the good—
(The Cross I know brings tolerance
  And teaches brotherhood).

This cross rekindles ancient hates
  That burned in alien lands—
(The Cross I know is stained with blood
  From nail-pierced, holy hands).

ADDIE M. HEDRICK

## The Suffering God

The cross they raised against the rain
  Of hideous boasts and cruel jeers
Bent down one head in human pain
  And lifted two old fears.

The one, a death that marked defeat,
  Laid darkness on the crying earth.
But in that darkness God could meet
  With men in their rebirth.

The other moved beneath the cross,
  A hidden fear that God might keep
Himself aloof—a visioned loss,
  That God could never weep.

Now darkness is dispelled with light
  Flaming the cross and the dark sky,
For God has suffered through this night
  And taught men how to die.

RAYMOND KRESENSKY

## Good Friday

Am I a stone, and not a sheep,
  That I can stand, O Christ, beneath Thy cross,
  To number drop by drop Thy Blood's slow loss,
And yet not weep?

Not so those women loved
   Who with exceeding grief lamented Thee;
   Not so fallen Peter weeping bitterly;
Not so the thief was moved;

Not so the Sun and Moon
   Which hid their faces in a starless sky.
   A horror of great darkness at broad noon—
I, only I.

Yet give not o'er
   But seek Thy sheep, true Shepherd of the flock;
   Greater than Moses, turn and look once more
And smite a rock.

                  CHRISTINA G. ROSSETTI


### "Two Others, on Either Side"

If I only had not chanced
   To come upon the way,
Where the bloody crosses branched
   In a fading day;

Had I only heard the tale,
   From mouth to mouth, of One
Dying by a bloody nail
   In a bloody sun—

I would never have the grim
   Haunting eyes to see;
Only the good eyes of him,
   Looking down at me;

*hadn't seen the Cross,
ever believe such
if it were possible*

I would never find the thief
  Where the saint has trod,
Trace a devil's harsh belief
  In a creed of God;

*using religion for evil
purposes*

I could lift a gilded cup,
  Snowy bread and wine,
Never asking, as I sup:
  "Is this mine?"

EDITH MIRICK

## Upon a Hill

Three men shared death upon a hill,
But only one man died;
The other two—
A thief and God himself—
Made rendezvous.

Three crosses still
Are borne up Calvary's Hill,
Where Sin lifts them high:
Upon the one sag broken men
Who, cursing, die;

Another holds the praying thief,
Or those who, penitent as he,
Still find the Christ
Beside them on the tree.

MIRIAM LeFEVRE CROUSE

### Calvary

A dying figure against the sky;
Laughter mocking a piteous cry;
Terror, silence, an anguished plea:
"Father, forgive them, they do not see!"

Piercing the darkness like singing flame,
"My Love shall enfold them!" the answer came.

MARY HALLET

### Gambler

And sitting down they watched him there,
The soldiers did;
There, while they played with dice,
He made his sacrifice,
And died upon the cross to rid
God's world of sin.
He was a gambler, too, my Christ,
He took his life and threw
It for a world redeemed.
And ere his agony was done,
Before the westering sun went down,
Crowning that day with crimson crown,
He knew that he had won.

G. A. STUDDERT-KENNEDY

### The Martyr

And all the while they mocked him and reviled,
And heaped upon him words of infamy;
He stood serenely there, and only smiled
In pity at the blind intensity
Of hate; for well he knew that Love alone
Can cure the ills of men—of nations, too—
Though unregenerate mobs their prophets stone,
And crucify the gentle Christ anew.
So he but smiled, and drained with quiet grace
The bitter cup for lips too eloquent,
And, dauntless, took the soul-degrading place
Designed for thieves—this Prophet heaven-sent!
And when the throng at length had hushed its cry,
Another cross loomed dark against the sky.

NATALIE FLOHR

### The Earth Worshiped!

A crown of thorns men gave to Christ,
　　Who should have worn the bay;
The wreath lay gently on his brow
　　And turned its points away.

"If thou be God," men mocking said,
　　"Then show to us a sign"—
They did not know the vinegar
　　Changed at his lips to wine.

The very earth's foundations shook,
  High heaven veiled its face;
Within a tomb sealed with a stone
  Men made the Lord a place.

The stone rolled outward at his word,
  The linen cloths untwined,
Earth had more reverence than men
  For him who saved mankind!
                    CATHERINE CATE COBLENTZ


## His Garments

He gave his life upon a cross;
  To those who hung him there
He gave forgiveness—and he left
  His clothes for them to wear!

That seamless vesture from whose hem
  Heaven's healing power stole
Was worn above a Roman heart!
  Oh, was that heart made whole?

Each hand that smote the thorn-crowned head,
  Each arm that drove a nail,
He covered with his raiment fair,
  And blood drops for them fell.

Was it I who pierced Thy side, my God,
  And looked upon Thee there?
White garments from Thy stainless life
  Oh give me, Lord, to wear!
                    ESTHER LLOYD HAGG

## The Ninth Hour

After the shameful trial in the hall,
The mocking and the scourging, and the pain
Of Peter's words; to Herod, and again
To Pilate's judgment seat, the royal pall,
The cross itself, the vinegar and gall;
The thieves close by, discipleship proved vain,
The scoffing crowd, his mother's tears like rain,
There came one moment, bitterest of all.
Yet in that cry, when flesh and spirit failed,
Last effort of the awful way he trod,
Which shook the earth, nor left the temple veiled,
In that exceeding great and bitter cry
Was conquest. The centurion standing by
Said, Truly this man was the Son of God.

CAROLINE HAZARD

## "Into Thy Hands"

Into Thy hands my spirit I commend;
From Thee it came and drave me to and fro,
Drave me to that to which I would not go.
Thou, its beginning, art its proper end;
I thirsted with a thirst men could not slake.
I drank the cup no other man could drink;
Thou didst sustain me, for I truly think
Mine was a loaf no other man could break.

Thou gavest me a vision of Thy church,
The power and the glory of Thy reign.
The vision dimmed; Caesar was there again:
Yet Spirit drave me to unending search.
And though the search has not achieved its end,
Into Thy hands my Spirit I commend.

LOREN W. BURCH

## Strength

Ask of your soul this question, What is strength?
   Is it to slay ten thousand with the sword?
To steal at midnight Gaza's brazen gates?
   To raze a temple on a heathen horde?

Or, in a garden drenched with evening dew
   And bloody sweat, to pray beside a stone?
Defend a sinner from self-righteous priests?
   Bear up to Calvary a cross, alone?

JESSIE WILMORE MURTON

## From "Christus"

My work is finished; I am strong
In faith, and hope, and charity;
For I have written the things I see,
The things that have been and shall be,
Conscious of right, nor fearing wrong;
Because I am in love with Love,
And the sole thing I hate is Hate;

For Hate is death; and Love is life,
A peace, a splendor from above;
And Hate, a never ending strife,
A smoke, a blackness from the abyss
Where unclean serpents coil and hiss!
Love is the Holy Ghost within;
Hate the unpardonable sin!
Who preaches otherwise than this
Betrays his Master with a kiss!

HENRY WADSWORTH LONGFELLOW

## Death of Christ

Pilate made report to Rome,
  Such as seemed worth while;
Sealed it, sent it off to Rome
  With a weary smile.

That was years and years ago—
  When the empire died
On a cross the Romans built
  Out of fear and pride.

ARTHUR R. MACDOUGALL, JR.

*Wonderful*

## Mary

Beside the empty sepulcher she lingered
   With tear-dimmed eyes, and heart with sorrow worn,
Nor heeded One whose presence in that garden
   A radiance shed, surpassing that of morn.

He stood beside her, though her eyes were holden,
   Then spoke her name, in accents low and sweet;
And at that long-loved voice she turned in rapture,
   Beheld her Lord, and worshiped at his feet.

So speak to us, dear Lord, amid earth's shadows,
   When doubts and fears oppress the human heart;
And at Thy voice shall break the light of morning,
   Revealing Thee, all-glorious as Thou art!

                       W. B.

## I Am the Cross

I am the Cross of Christ.
I bore his body there
   On Calvary's lonely hill.
Till then I was a humble tree
   That grew beside a tiny rill;
I think till then
I was a thing despised of men!

I am the Cross of Christ!
I felt his limbs along

My common, broken bark;
I saw his utter loneliness,
   The lightning and the dark;
And up till then
I thought he was as other men.

I am the Cross of Christ!
My form they used to crucify
   The outcasts of the earth;
But on that lonely hill that day
   My kind received, in blood, new birth,
And ever till this day
A weary world bows at my feet to pray!

I am the Cross of Christ.
They say I tower "o'er the wrecks
Of time." I only know
That once, a humble tree,
This was not so. But this
I know—since then
I have become a symbol for the hopes of men.

                    WILLIAM L. STIDGER

### Conquest        X

Though rulers spend a million men
   For gain or loss,
Yet One had need for only twelve,
   And for a cross.

              LESLIE SAVAGE CLARK

### Dereliction
*"Eloi, eloi, lama sabacthani"*

I have seen morning break within his eyes
  That caught the heavenly light;
And I have seen in him the midnight skies,
  The very night of night.

I have seen God within that morning glow;
  But not before his cry,
*My God, why hast Thou left me?* did I know
  That God could be so nigh.

The shrine was brightest with the lamp withdrawn;
  His winter was my spring;
His midnight cry the voices of my dawn;
  The Crucified, my King!

EDWARD SHILLITO

### Revealment

They planned for Christ a cruel death;
  Steel pierced his hands, and feet and side;
They mocked his last expiring breath,
  And thought their hate was satisfied.

They wagged their heads and said, "Lo, he
  Would crush our temple and in three days
Restore its beauty. Come and see
  This boaster gone death's quiet ways."

They did not know that on that hill
  Eternal love was satisfied;        *not justice, or revenge.*
That Christ, who hung there, triumphed still.
. . . And only cruel death had died!
                    JOHN RICHARD MORELAND


### His Hands

  The hands of Christ
    Seem very frail,
  For they were broken
    By a nail.

  But only they reach
    Heaven at last
  Whom these frail, broken
    Hands hold fast.
                JOHN RICHARD MORELAND

## The Syrian's Tale

While riding toward Jerusalem
  Across the gloomy hill
Where once a traitor hung himself
  I saw one, limp and still.
The moonlight lay like silver coins
  Around that gruesome place;
I shudder yet remembering
  The anguish on his face.

When I had left Jerusalem
  By Calvary, grim and bare,
I saw three crosses on the hill
  And men were hanging there.
And one was young and glorious
  With strangely royal grace;
I marvel yet remembering
  The light upon his face.

LESLIE SAVAGE CLARK

## There Was a Man

There was a man—or was he but a man?—
Who walked alone with God. Though at his side
Walked other men, they could not know his dreams;
They scorned his lofty words. His eye could scan
The secrets of the stars, and lo! they cried,
"This man is mad!" But, blinded by the gleams
Of dawning glory, still he loved and sang.

He sang of beauty, sang of faith and hope,
And little children gladly heard his songs.
But men—though all the bells of heaven rang
With joy of him—they could but blindly grope.
They railed upon him, took brute whips with thongs,
And foully beat him. Him at last they slew,
Who, dying, cried: "They know not what they do."

THOMAS CURTIS CLARK

### There Is a Man on the Cross

Whenever there is silence around me
By day or by night—
I am startled by a cry.
It came down from the cross—
The first time I heard it.
I went out and searched—
And found a man in the throes of crucifixion,
And I said, "I will take you down,"
And I tried to take the nails out of his feet.
But he said, "Let them be
For I cannot be taken down
Until every man, every woman, and every child
Come together to take me down."
And I said, "But I cannot hear you cry.
What can I do?"
And he said, "Go about the world—
Tell everyone that you meet—
There is a man on the cross."

ELIZABETH CHENEY

## Kingdoms

The kingdoms of the earth go by
    In purple and in gold:
They rise, they flourish, and they die,
    And all their tale is told.
One kingdom only is divine,
    One banner triumphs still:
Its king a servant, and its sign
    A gibbet on a hill.

ANONYMOUS

*"My kingdom is not of this world"*

## Calvary

If he could doubt on his triumphal cross,
How much more I, in the defeat and loss
Of seeing all my selfish dreams fulfilled,
Of having lived the very life I willed,
Of being all that I desired to be?
My God, my God! Why hast Thou forsaken me?

WILLIAM DEAN HOWELLS

*The despair of having lived all your life just as you desire.*

## Judge Me, O Lord!

If I had been in Palestine
A poor disciple I had been.
I had not risked or purse or limb
All to forsake, and follow Him.

*We were there when they crucified our Lord — ? we*

But with the vast and wondering throng
I too had stood and listened long;
I too had felt my spirit stirred
When the Beatitudes I heard.

With the glad crowd that sang the psalm,
I too had sung, and strewed the palm;
Then slunk away in dastard shame
When the High Priest denounced His name.
But when my late companions cried
"Away! Let Him be crucified!"
I would have begged, with tremulous
Pale lips, "Release Him unto us!"

Beside the cross when Mary prayed,
A great way off I too had stayed;
Not even in that hour had dared,
And for my dying Lord declared,
But beat upon my craven breast,
And loathed my coward heart, at least,
To think my life I dared not stake
And beard the Romans for His sake.

SARAH N. CLEGHORN

## For Me

Under an Eastern sky,
Amid a rabble cry,
A man went forth to die,
For me!

Thorn-crowned his blessed head,
Blood-stained his every tread,
Cross-laden on he sped,
  For me!

Pierced glow his hands and feet,
Three hours o'er him did beat
Fierce rays of noontide heat,
  For me!

Thus wert Thou made all mine;
Lord, make me wholly Thine,
Give grace and strength divine,
  To me!

In thought and word and deed,
Thy will to do; oh, lead my feet
E'en though they bleed,
  To Thee!
      ANONYMOUS

### Litany

*wonderful.*

Oh, by Thy cross and passion, by Thy pain,
Thy resurrection and eternal reign,
From blindness of the soul whose certain doom
Is death, ere yet we molder in the tomb,
 *Deliver us!*

From love that cannot see beyond the grave,
However tender, or however brave,

But would—as if this pilgrimage were all—
The ointment bring, the winding-sheet, the pall,
  *Deliver us!*

Remember not, we pray, our foolish ways,
The fear, the doubt that move us still to raise
Walls around Thee who loved the hungry crowds—
But shame us with Thine own discarded shrouds,
  *O Lamb of God!*

Life, Life and ever more abundant Life!
Bread of Thy flesh to man us in the strife,
Wine of Thy blood and fervor of Thy flame
Give us to dream, dare, triumph in Thy Name,
  *O Lamb of God!*

MARIE LeNART

### Dying

Beauty goes out to meet a greater beauty,
  Something we cannot grasp, who cry our loss—
Something God meant when he made the first morning,
Something *He* meant, who stumbled with a cross!

JESSIE HOLT

### What Will the Stars Remember?

What will the stars remember
  After the earth is gone,
What dreams will they carry with them
  Into a nobler dawn?

*never forgotten*

A man who flung, unflinching,
  A truth against a lie,
A dog at the grave of his master, *Edinburgh.*
  And a Cross against the sky.

LILITH LORRAINE

## Waking Thought

*cross*

*God gives light thru the Cross*

Waking I look to Jesus on the Rood
  And thank him that the ghostly night is gone;
Until my soul had seen the Holy Cross
  I never knew the dawn.

All colors were as darkness save the hues
  That even our dull bodily eyes can see,
But now is God grown fair beyond the East   *universal*
  Upon his blessed tree.      *beauty*

MARGUERITE WILKINSON

## The Cross

So heavy and so fraught with pain,
But I must bravely trudge along
The dusty way . . . nor dare arraign
My cross.

I have no voice to lift in song;
When sorrow's recompense I feign
The muffled notes of grief remain.

And yet he prayed for strength to drain
The bitter dregs and bear the thong.
His kingly soul did not disdain
The cross.

SHIRLEY DILLON WAITE

### Jesus of the Scars

*[handwritten: X Only our God suffered for us — not gods of myths]*

If we never sought, we seek Thee now;
  Thine eyes burn through the dark, our only stars;
We must have sight of thorn-pricks on Thy brow,
  We must have Thee, O Jesus of the Scars.

The heavens frighten us; they are too calm;
  In all the universe we have no place.
Our wounds are hurting us; where is the balm?
  Lord Jesus, by Thy Scars we claim Thy grace.

*[handwritten: Here is a clue to suffering]*

If when the doors are shut, Thou drawest near,
  Only reveal those hands, that side of Thine;
We know today what wounds are, have no fear,
  Show us Thy Scars, we know the countersign.

The other gods were strong; but Thou wast weak;
  They rode, but Thou didst stumble to a throne;
But to our wounds only God's wounds can speak,
  And not a god has wounds, but Thou alone.

EDWARD SHILLITO

## Crusts

How cruel they! the cause of all
    His anguish—they who gibed and cursed;
Then proffered cup of bitter gall
    To slake his thirst.

Yet we, who set ourselves apart,
    Still nourish sordid greed and lust:
He hungers for a loving heart;
    We fling—a crust.

WALTER SHEA

## E Tenebris

Come down, O Christ, and help me! reach thy hand,
For I am drowning in a stormier sea
Than Simon on thy lake of Galilee:
The wine of life is spilt upon the sand,
My heart is as some famine-murdered land
Whence all good things have perished utterly,
And well I know my soul in Hell must lie
If I this night before God's throne should stand.
"He sleeps perchance, or rideth to the chase,
Like Baal, when his prophets howled that name
From morn to noon on Carmel's smitten height."
Nay, peace, I shall behold, before the night,
The feet of brass, the robe more white than flame,
The wounded hands, the weary human face.

OSCAR WILDE

### The Cup

If now unto my lips be raised
   The brimming cup of bitter gall,
Grant Thy great strength, dear Lord, and I
   Will drink it all.

My lips may quiver, and my faint heart quail,
   And I may cry at its dread call;
Hold Thou my hand, dear Lord, and I
   Will drink it all.

FREDERICK T. ROBERTS

### Good Friday

Gall is the taste of life when we
Who live must bear our Calvary.
On this day our Master died—
Christ, our Lord, the Crucified.
Upon the cross in agony
He shed his blood for love of me.
In every street, on every hill,
The Heart that stopped is beating still.

VINCENT HOLME

### Interpretation

The cross that bears my Master slain—
Is it a sign to me that I
Am spared the toil, the shame, the pain,
Or on a cross like him should die?

SHELDON SHEPARD

### Unity

Jesus,
Wracked on your cross,
Let me draw out the spikes. . . .
*No, my son, not until all men
Help you.*

LLOYD FRANK MERRELL

### The Stranger

I saw him where the rose was red
Pressing the cruel thorns between
His hands until his pale palms bled,
As he walked through my garden-space
And on his face
Such sorrow as I had not seen.

"Sad Stranger, who are you that walk
Where loveliness has birth?

Why are your palms all torn and dark?"
He broke another rose blood-red
And turned and said:
"Yourself stripped of your mask of mirth." *Jake*

JOHN RICHARD MORELAND

## A Certain Saturday

Lost day
When hope was sealed in its integument.
Day of dark gestation.
Nameless day
Slipping quietly between the drama of a Friday
And the glory of a Sunday.
Rest, pause, muted time-beat,
Symbol of so many of our days
Wherein we only grow invisibly,
Wherein we only climb and do not know it.
Day torn between the grasping hands
Of the past and the future.
Aerial hollow nestling between the two flaming wings
Of a sunset and a sunrise.

EDITH LOVEJOY PIERCE

*Cross as Symbol* (handwritten margin note)

## From "The Cathedral"

. . . . Whatsoe'er
The form of building or the creed professed,
The Cross, bold type of shame to homage turned,
Of an unfinished life that sways the world,
Shall tower as sovereign emblem over all.

JAMES RUSSELL LOWELL

## From "Karshish"

So, the All-Great were the All-Loving too—
So, through the thunder comes a human voice
Saying, "O heart I made, a heart beats here!
Face, my hands fashioned, see it in myself.
Thou hast no power nor may'st conceive of mine,
But love I gave thee, with myself to love,
And thou must love me who have died for thee!"

ROBERT BROWNING

*Incarnation* (handwritten margin note)

*The far off God is intimate* (handwritten margin note)

*The Being — has a heart a face, & love. His power is beyond us — but we can love Him* (handwritten note)

*Rich, became poor.* (handwritten note)

## My Master

My Master was so very poor,
A manger was His cradling place;
So very rich my Master was
Kings came from far
To gain His grace.

My Master was so very poor
And with the poor He broke the bread;
So very rich my Master was
That multitudes
By Him were fed.

My Master was so very poor
They nailed Him naked to a cross;
So very rich my Master was
He gave His all
And knew no loss.

HARRY LEE

## From "Of Our Lord's Passion"

In Thine hour of holy sadness
Could I share with Thee, what gladness
Should Thy cross to me be showing.
Gladness past all thought of knowing,
    Bowed beneath Thy cross to die!

Blessed Jesus, thanks I render
That in bitter death, so tender,
Thou dost hear Thy suppliant calling;
Save me, Lord, and keep from falling
    From Thee, when mine hour is nigh.

BERNARD OF CLAIRVAUX

### The Cross

Charlemagne carried it far
   Into a pagan fight;
Constantine gilded it like a star
   To glow on the breast of night,
High on an ancient dome,
   Where eyes of tired men turn;
Low on a marble tomb,
   By fading flowers of an urn.

Prelates linked it to a chain,
   The symbol of love, of power—
But only One of us would deign
   To bleed on it for an hour.
Only Christ, of the sons of men,
   Shouldered it for a loss,
Stripped of its glamor scarlet sin,
   And died with it, on a cross.

           RUBY WEYBURN TOBIAS

### The Rich Young Man

It seemed so mad a thing to do—
To grieve so deep—to perish, too
For men He never even knew!
A life so lonely, meek, and bare!
I wonder why He made a prayer
For them that mocked and nailed Him there!

Vast wealth is mine; why do I see
My golden hoard without avail?
Why turns no man with love to me?
Why did He triumph, and I fail?
Poor and despised! how strange a thing
That mighty hosts, with worshipping,
Their homage to His name should bring!

Oh, 'tis a grievous mystery—
That mankind never looks to me
As to that spent and broken Christ
That drooped on Calvary!

LAURA SIMMONS

## Immunity

Think you to escape
What mortal man can never be without?
What saint upon earth has ever lived apart from cross and
    care?
Why, even Jesus Christ, our Lord, was not even for one
    hour free from his passion's pain.
Christ says, "He needs must suffer,
Rising from the dead,
And enter thus upon his glory."
And how do *you* ask for another road
Than this—the Royal Pathway of the Holy Cross?

THOMAS À KEMPIS

*[handwritten marginalia: "life without cross impossible" and "Sermon topic"]*

### Crucifixion *with Xst*

"Lord, must I bear the whole of it, or none?"
"Even as I was crucified, My son."

"Will it suffice if I the thorn-crown wear?"
"To take the scourge, My shoulders were made to bear."

"My hands, O Lord, must I be pierced in both?"
"Twain gave I to the hammer, nothing loth."

"But surely, Lord, my feet need not be nailed?"
"Had Mine not been, then love had not prevailed."

"What need I more, O Lord, to fill my part?"
"Only the spear-point in a broken heart."

FREDERICK GEORGE SCOTT

### Not Yours But You

He died for me: what can I offer him?
Toward him swells incense of perpetual prayer;
His court wear crowns and aureoles round their hair;
His ministers are subtle Cherubim;
Ring within ring, white intense Seraphim
Leap like immortal lightnings through the air.
What shall I offer him? Defiled and bare
My spirit broken and my brightness dim?
"Give Me thy youth." "I yield it to Thy rod,
As Thou didst yield Thy prime of youth for me."

"Give Me thy life." "I give it breath by breath;
As Thou didst give Thy life so give I Thee."
"Give Me thy love." "So be it, my God, my God,
As Thou hast loved me, even to bitter death."

CHRISTINA G. ROSSETTI


## O Christ, Who Died

O Christ, who died upon a cross,
My soul attests your sharpest pain:
'Twas not the spikes in hands or feet,
'Twas not the spearthrust in your side;
These were but instruments of death,
From which your spirit never winced.
No, Lord, the sword that thrust you through
Was in the hands of faithless friends;
Their gross indifference to your fate
Was sharper than the keenest blade.
To know that those you trusted most
Had failed you in your darkest hour—
That was the stroke that pierced your heart
And brought release to death's grim power.

O Christ, whose cross is ever new,
Alas, it must be so today,
As friends of yours still stand apart
And let you die with bleeding heart.

JOHN CALVIN SLEMP

## Holier Night

A star looked down on Bethlehem;
　In silver radiance swam
Those quiet fields where shepherds watched
　Beside the new-born lamb.

No star looked down on Calvary,
　Upon that lonely sod
Dark with the blood of sacrifice—
　O Lamb of God!

Leslie Savage Clark

## The Way of the World

The hands of the King are soft and fair
　They never knew labor's strain.
The hands of the Robber redly wear
　The bloody brand of Cain.
But the hands of the Man are hard and scarred
　With the scars of toil and pain.

The slaves of Pilate have washed his hands
　As white as a king's might be.
Barabbas with wrists unfettered stands
　For the world has made him free.
But Thy palms toil-worn by nails are torn,
　O Christ, on Calvary.

James Jeffrey Roche

free the world
free the condemned
& condemn the
free

p 150

### The Centurion
#### (*A Vision*)

I saw him leave his pagan century
By stealth, to trail a ruffian mob by night,
And in the circle of a lanthorn's light,
Within the garden called Gethsemane,
Behold in pained bewilderment, the sight
Of Innocence ensnared by treachery . . .
As at a later hour he stood to see
The Sacrifice upon Golgotha's height.

But when he came to call the drunken guard
Sleep-drowned on duty at a vacant tomb,
And saw a thousand lilies gem the sward
Where Jesus walked unfettered in the gloom,
His pale lips smitten by an angel's rod,
Cried out, "I know this is the Son of God!"

HELEN PURCELL ROADS

### Of Things Not Seen

Theirs is the courage of flesh and bone—
The wolf, though crippled, leaps
At the hunter's throat; in a trail of blood

The wounded tiger creeps
After his foe. Yet man, alone,
Shall count as naught the loss
Of all he holds, for hemlock cup,
Faggot . . . Cross!

LESLIE SAVAGE CLARK

*Tremendous — "Take up Thy Cross: follow Me"*

## Calvary

Five thousand followed him for fish and loaves,
But only twelve when he broke beauty's bread;
So is it still when a free spirit roves
Over the earth wherever he may tread.
How many blindly worship him who sought
Only for truth and loveliness, who broke
The unjust usages of time, and thought
The rebel thought in him until it spoke!
Yet they who dare a lonely fate—how few
In some Gethsemane beneath the stars,
While the five thousand seek a cushioned pew
And ask for ease, not beauty with its scars!
O You who loved the lilies and the sea,
They have their creed, and You your Calvary.

HUGH ROBERT ORR

*Jesus spoke rebel truth*

## Simon and Judas

At these two men well may we churchmen scoff—
We who have struck not once with any sword,
Who have so many times betrayed our Lord,
Nor followed even at a great way off!

KENNETH W. PORTER

## Entrance Into Heaven

*X Stephen*

Down the white steps of Heaven Christ came to meet him,
  That soul with rope-galled throat, and stricken eyes;
Hastened with glad and outstretched hands to greet him,
  And led him proudly into Paradise.

*To Judas*

Christ said: "Thou, too, hast known Gethsemane,
  Condemned for what the world accounted not
Obedience! That shame required of thee,
  Wilt thou forgive, my friend Iscariot?"

SARA HENDERSON HAY

*cf Acts 4*

*Judas had to do it for God's purposes to be carried out*

## Legacy

My Lord, when he went back—
  Back to the glory of that sunlit throne
He had left empty for a little while,
My Lord, when he went back

Left no estate. The only things he had
Were garments which men gambled on,
And one good robe "made without seam throughout,"
The watching soldiers each for this cast lots.
For legacy he left his Mother and his friend,
And each was well content.

RUTH WINANT WHEELER

## Were Flowers There?

I wonder—were there flowers there
On Calvary that fateful day?
In that green sod, from which the rude cross
Thrust aloft—(Love's bitter pay!)—
Did wise old Nature show the late-spilt blood
Of purple violet bloom,
That took a deeper and a darker hue
Amid the shadowed gloom?
Did scarlet stain of spring's anemone
Or crimson flush of rose
Give grace to scene of sin's brutality
And Love's redeeming throes?
Did lilies bloom on bending stems
In flowered white with heart of gold?
Or were there only thorn-trees, cacti,
And rocks—as gray as they were old?

GEORGE WILLIAM ALLISON

### The Passion Flower

Thou lowly, meek and lovely flower,
But yesterday, at evening's hour,
As trudged I upward with my load,
I saw thee blooming by the road,
And stayed my steps to wonder there
That beauty so supremely fair
Should waste its loveliness on me—
Even as the Flower of Calvary!

CHARLES G. BLANDEN


### Question

I wonder if that cypress tree
  Which stood in Eden long ago
And lifted hands where bird and bee
  Winged heaven through the season's flow,
Was ever mindful that a day
  Would bring it aching agony,
And it would stand, a cross, to slay
  The Christ of love on Calvary.

HOWARD McKINLEY CORNING

*The Tree made sacred*

### The Cross and the Tree

A tree is such a sacred thing;
  I never knew just why
Until I saw my Saviour, Christ,
  Stretched on a tree to die;
And heard him lift his pleading voice
  In one great tender cry.

And now I know why poets sing
  About a common tree
As if it were a sacred thing
  Of God-like destiny;
As if each stalwart oak had roots
  That reached to Calvary!

             WILLIAM L. STIDGER

### Song

What trees were in Gethsemane,
  What flowers were there to scent,
When Christ for you, and Christ for me,
  Into his garden went?

The fragrant cedar tree was there,
  The lily pale and slim:
They saw his grief, they heard his prayer,
  And wept their dews for him.

*as symbols still fit*

And that is why the cedars green
  And why the lilies white
Do whisper of the Master's love
  In gardens, late at night.

CHARLES G. BLANDEN

## The Tragedy

He gave the world, in darkness pent,
  The boon of his surpassing light;
The world found healing in its beams,
  But turned him out into the night.

He gave the world his heart of hearts,
  And bore the burden of its woe;
The world gave him the knotted scourge,
  The cruel rod's remorseless blow.

He gave the world the hope of heaven,
  And to its gates the wanderers led;
The thankless world could not find room
  Where he might lay his weary head.

He gave the world the crown of life,
  His life accounting but as dross;
The world received the matchless gift,
  And gave to him the martyr's cross!

THOMAS CURTIS CLARK

*Matt 28 "authority"*
*Jno.*

## Who Can Forget?

This is the greatest proof of power—
   The strength to lay it down.
The dust of centuries lies deep
   Upon the once-proud crown
Of Nineveh or Babylon;
   Though few remember them,
Who can forget a lonely hill
   Outside Jerusalem?

                    LESLIE SAVAGE CLARK

## From "What of the Night?"

Arrogant Kings, with envious lust
For power, impress on things of dust
Proud images. Small coins of brass
Show forth their face as in a glass,
While superscriptions boast their name,
The years they ruled, their weight of fame.
Only one King has shed his blood
That men might walk in brotherhood:
Whose coin is love, and graved thereon
A scourge, a cross, a crown of thorn!

                    JOHN RICHARD MORELAND

## Last Hill

You who have raised
   And bound me high
Fast to a cross
   And think I die,

Tortured by ills,
   The nail and thirst:
Death of the man,
   Despised, accurst:

Little you know
   I died in sweet
Circle of beauty,
   Cool, complete;

Little you know
   I died that night;
Died from a kiss
   By lantern light.
          EDITH MIRICK

## The Great Wager

How is it proved?
It isn't proved, you fool; it can't be proved.
How can you prove a victory before
It's won? How can you prove a man who leads

To be a leader worth the following,
Unless you follow to the death, and out
Beyond mere death, which is not anything
But Satan's lie upon eternal life?
Well—God's my leader, and I hold that he
Is good, and strong enough to work his plan
And purpose out to its appointed end.

I walk in crowded streets, where men
And women, mad with lust, loose-lipped, and lewd,
Go promenading down to hell's wide gates;
Yet have I looked into my mother's eyes
And seen the light that never was on sea
Or land, the light of love, pure love and true,
And on that love I bet my life. . . .

. . . I bet my life on beauty, truth,
And love! not abstract, but incarnate truth;
Not beauty's passing shadow, but its self,
Its very self made flesh—love realized.
I bet my life on Christ, Christ crucified.

                              G. A. STUDDERT-KENNEDY

### I Have Overcome the World

The crown of empire—must thou yield it now?
(Mine was of thorns they pressed upon My brow.)

Did friends, as foes, desert thee in thy power?
(Mine could not watch with Me one single hour.)

Is all thy life stripped stark through shame and loss?
(Between two thieves I hung upon a cross.)

LAURA SIMMONS

### From "The Veteran of Heaven"

O Captain of the wars, whence won Ye so great scars?
In what fight did Ye smite, and what manner was the foe?
Was it on a day of rout they compassed Thee about,
Or gat Ye these adornings when Ye wrought their over-
    throw?

" 'Twas on a day of rout they girded Me about,
They wounded all My brow, and they smote Me through
    the side:
My hand held no sword when I met their armèd horde,
And the conqueror fell down, and the Conquered bruised *Gen 3¹⁵*
    his pride."

FRANCIS THOMPSON

### I Saw Death Slain

Call me no more the cursèd tree
    Because I was compelled to play
A part in that great tragedy
    When darkness veiled the face of day.

'Twas not decreed by cruel Fate
    That I of all the trees should be
The instrument with which man's hate
    Might torture Christ on Calvary.

I felt with Jesus each harsh nail
    That pierced his tender hands and feet;
Yet never knight with sword and mail
    Was armed as he the foe to meet.

For he was girded with the power
    That guides the myriad stars above
And paints the petals of each flower—
    The all-prevailing power of Love.

I held up Christ that men might see
    The meaning of the tragedy.
Call me henceforth the blessed tree—
    I saw Death slain on Calvary.

WILLIAM CAPELL

*Trevordore* X

## Prayer of a Modern Thomas    *God in Xst died*

If Thou, O God, the Christ didst leave,
In him, not Thee, I do believe;
    To Jesus dying, all alone,
    To his dark Cross, not Thy bright Throne,
My hopeless hands will cleave.

But if it was Thy love that died,
Thy voice that in the darkness cried,
    The print of nails I long to see;
    In Thy hands, God, who fashioned me,
Show me Thy piercèd side.

EDWARD SHILLITO

## Quatrain

Christ bears a thousand crosses now
    Where once but one he bore;
Each cruel deed unto his brow
    Adds one thorn more.

CHARLES G. BLANDEN

## The Cross

X *our symbols fall far short of the real.*

A cross? That?
That shapely, smooth-wrought thing of shimmering gold,
That lovely, polished mass so finely tooled,

Clean, straight, symmetrical, beautiful,
In the dim religious light upon the altar—
   That, a cross?

The cross!
Against a darkening sky, three crosses!
Rough-hewn, sharp-edged, splintery;
No studied elegance nor smoothness there,
But nails, and tearing flesh, and blood!
Ah, God, blood, and agony, and death!
   The cross—beautiful?
   That—a cross?

CHARLES S. BRADEN

# The Continuing Calvary

# The Continuing Calvary

## Good Friday

I for thy sake was pierced with heavy sorrow,
   And bore the cross,
Yet heeded not the sharpness of the arrow,
   Nor shame and loss.

So faint not thou, whate'er the burden be,
But bear it bravely, even to Calvary.

GIROLAMO SAVONAROLA

## Ave Crux, Spes Unica!

More than two crosses stand on either side
   The Cross today on more than one dark hill;
More than three hours a myriad men have cried,
   And they are crying still.

Before him now no mocking faces pass;
    Heavy on all who built the cross, it lies;
Pilate is hanging there, and Caiaphas,
    Judas without his price.

Men scourge each other with their stinging whips;
    To crosses high they nail, and they are nailed;
More than one dying man with parchèd lips,
    "My God! My God!" has wailed.

Enlarged is Golgotha. But One alone
    His healing shadow over all can fling;
One King divine has made his Cross a Throne.
    "Remember us, O King!"

                 EDWARD SHILLITO

## Golgotha

They did not crucify the Lord
    One time alone.
For I have seen him on a tree;
Have watched him bleed and die for me,
And, mocking at his agony,
    Have also thrown a stone.

The skull-shaped hill called Golgotha
    Is not one place.
In factory, mill and farming plain,
Where women's bodies sell for gain,
And children's souls are warped in pain
    I see his tortured face.

Lord, when we bend the knee before Thy throne,
How shall we answer, who have slain Thine own?

KATHERINE GREENLEAF PEDLEY

### Atonement

Atonement? Lord, who doth atone today?
  Uplifted on the cross, canst Thou not see
Atonement died somewhere along the way
  Between the tomb and dark Gethsemane?

*the Cross of 33 A.D. is not still forgiving*

Thine be the hyssop and the bitter draught,
  Thine be the anguish and the ridicule:
They were not all at Calvary who laughed—
  The knave, the soldier, Pharisee and fool!

*you still suffer*

They were not all at Calvary who bid
  Their tawdry baubles for Thy seamless robe,
Or, while the very sun its radiance hid,
  The spear upraised, Thy tortured flesh to probe.

And yet, dear Lord, a few keep watch with Thee,
  A few Thy truth with earnest hearts still seek,
Like those who slumbered through Thine agony—
  The spirit willing, though the flesh be weak.

*the church*

And so, with traitor, thief and Magdalene,
  In Thine immortal prayer include us too,
And by the sacrifice that maketh clean
  Forgive us—we know not what we do!

MARIE LENART

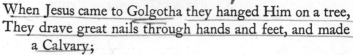

## Indifference

When Jesus came to Golgotha they hanged Him on a tree,
They drave great nails through hands and feet, and made
    a Calvary;
They crowned Him with a crown of thorns, red were His
    wounds and deep,
For those were crude and cruel days, and human flesh
    was cheap.

When Jesus came to Birmingham, they simply passed Him
    by,
They never hurt a hair of Him, they only let Him die;
For men had grown more tender, and they would not give
    Him pain,
They only just passed down the street, and left Him in
    the rain.

Still Jesus cried, "Forgive them, for they know not what
    they do,"
And still it rained the winter rain that drenched Him
    through and through;
The crowds went home and left the streets without a soul
    to see,
And Jesus crouched against a wall and cried for Calvary.

                   G. A. STUDDERT-KENNEDY

*He preferred the Cross —
to sheer indifference*

### Daily Cross

Calvary was just one more
 Cross on which the Master died,
By loneliness and all men's woes
 Daily crucified.

Daily dying steeled his soul
 To triumph over one more death
And tyrannies he had defied,
 With each rebellious breath.
                    EARL BIGELOW BROWN

*[handwritten: X True, Inspired He went daily to the Cross. In essence]*

*[handwritten: X good        Social Gospel.]*

### "Except Ye Repent"

Christ, forgive us!
We paste the label of your name    *[handwritten: Christian]*
On deeds and attitudes
Whose like you bitterly condemned,
Paying for your fearlessness
Upon a cross of wood.

Christ, awake us!
Face us with the truth. The outer show
Means nothing in the eyes of God
If we condone the wrong within.
God does not read the labels.

Christ, pity us!
We give the sacred name of "Christian"
To manufacturer and merchant,
Paying bills for churchly ritual
And talking unctuously of brotherhood,
While workers take starvation wage
Or hunger, unemployed.

Christ, pray for us!
"Father, forgive them. They know not what they do."
Repeat the words of old,
While, crucified afresh, you hang
Upon the cross of greed.

J. FRANKLIN PINEO

## Fellowship

Caiaphas, Pilate and Herod—
   How we despise each name!
They sent the Blessed to the cross,
   And hung him, to their shame.

But you and I, and you and I,
   Partakers of their deed,
Go blithely on as righteous men,
   Unscathed by human need.

No nailprints mutilate our hands,
   No sword wounds pierce the side.
We do not have the mark of thorns;
   O Lord, forgive our pride!

Send nails to pin us to Thy cross,
  Send swords to cleave us through.
Let brothers' sufferings pierce like thorns,
  Until we bleed—with You!
                    ELINOR LENNEN


## Three Crosses

Three crosses stood on Calvary
  Stark against the sky.
Roman soldiers laughed to see
  Three ways a man may die.

Crosses still stand on Calvary
  Stark against the sky,
And some still laugh to see
  Men die . . . hear little children cry.

Who builds the cross on Calvary
  Stark against the sky?
Who laughs at pain and want?
  Can it be you—or I?
        LEILA AVERY ROTHENBURGER


## Not All the Crosses

Not all the crosses are on hills
  Against a livid sky,
Not all the riven hands are scarred,
  Nor all the pierced hearts die!

We face a thousand little deaths
  That none may see or guess
What searing wounds we hide beneath
  Our body's loveliness.

The little song that missed its way,
  Love, patient and unclaimed,
Old scornful words whose memory
  Still turns us sick and shamed;

A smile that flicked a scorpion lash,
  Gray eyes that did not heed,
The friend beloved and leaned upon
  Who failed us in our need.

Not all the crosses are on hills—
  And oh, God, keep in sight
Those who come down from Calvary
  With hands unscarred and white!
                LUCILE KENDRICK

### Follow Me!

In the name of Him who died
  They kick against the pricks
And bow in selfish pride
  Before the crucifix,
With holy water laved.
  O will they never see
That only those are saved
  Who hang upon the tree!
                SHELDON SHEPARD

## Crucifixion

Had I been there that cruel day
  When Jesus hung upon the cross,
I would have shouted loud the shame
  And fought with no regard for loss.

But let me think—was it today
  A name was slandered in our town,
When I stood by nor raised a hand
  To put the smooth-tongued liars down?

Had I been there I might have watched
  With mute consent the dark hours through . . .
Forgive me, Lord, for worse than they
  I kill and know well what I do.

CARL S. WEIST

*[handwritten margin note: We crucify — innocence — we are ashamed to defend truth]*

## The Greater Guilt

They gave his flesh the sting of knout,
  His silence, shout and scorn,
They gave his kingliness a reed,
  And crowned his head with thorn.

They gave his body to the cross,
  His anguish, jest and jeer,
They gave his thirst but vinegar,
  His breaking heart, a spear.

This happened centuries ago,
  But still, today, we treat him so!

JOHN RICHARD MORELAND

### A Follower

I might have climbed up Calvary
 With willing steps, though slow,
And found the way less steep to me
 Than feet reluctant know.

I might have held the cooling cup,
 To lips grown gray with pain,
And in the act of looking up
 Known agony as gain.

Instead, I feel myself to be,
 Through shame and conscious loss,
One Simon of Cyrene—
 Compelled to bear my cross.
     Daisy Conway Price

*[handwritten note: have learned to Calvary — that we gain only comes thru suffering.]*


### Intolerance

*[handwritten note: mystic vision of crucifixion]*

A jet form swaying in the morning mist
Naked and bleeding. Still the heart of man
Is either Pharisee or Puritan—
Lover of creed more than it loves the Christ!
     John Richard Moreland

## The Second Coming

Christ came to earth again, and made his plea
To hosts who honored what they thought was he . . .
A shout arose; once more a crucifix
Showed a torn figure nailed upon a tree.

STANTON A. COBLENTZ

## I Sought the Living God

I sought the living God in ancient lore,
O'er time-worn creeds I pored expectantly;
But through the years there came no surety,
The far-off goal was distant as before.
At shrines, in temples then I sped my quest;
I followed aimless paths where'er they led;
But still there was no pillow for my head,
No shelter from the storm, no place of rest.

At length, quite spent, I heard a jeering mob
In frenzy shouting, "Hang him! String him up!"
I thought of Calvary, its bitter cup;
I saw the victim praying, heard him sob.
Then, God, that moment stood I by Thy side:
I saw Thee suffer in the Crucified.

JOHN CALVIN SLEMP

### Free Enterprise

Three workmen fashioning a cross
   On which a fourth must die!
Yet none of any other asked,
   "And why? And why? And why?"

Said they: "This is our business,
   Our living we must earn;
What happens to the other man
   Is none of our concern!"

CLYDE McGEE

### Holy Week

I cannot wax ecstatic with the throng
Of parasites and servitors, who pray
And make such vast ado, this week and day,
Over the details of an ancient wrong,
Yet in their soddenness themselves prolong
Still, for the son of man, Golgotha's way;
Who yet the slaving multitudes betray,
That they may share in Herod's dance and song.
I count remembrance of the martyred dead
Remembrance only worthy of esteem
When it bears onward still the martyr's dream
And dares like protest for the common good.
They who stand well today with Caesar's brood
Call me in vain; so much they leave unsaid.

ROBERT WHITAKER

## After the Martyrdom

They threw a stone, you threw a stone,
   I threw a stone that day.
Although their sharpness bruised His flesh
   He had no word to say.

But for the moan He did not make
   Today I make my moan;
And for the stone I threw at Him
   My heart must bear a stone.

SCHARMEL IRIS

## The Question

I saw the Son of God go by
   Crowned with the crown of thorn.
"Was it not finished, Lord?" I said,
   "And all the anguish borne?"

He turned on me his awful eyes:
   "Hast thou not understood?
Lo! Every soul is Calvary,
   And every sin a Rood."

RACHEL ANNAND TAYLOR

*cf. Weatherhead*

### Christ Is Crucified Anew

Not only once, and long ago,
There on Golgotha's side,
Has Christ, the Lord, been crucified
Because He loved a lost world so.
But hourly souls, sin-satisfied,
Mock His great love, flout His commands.
And I drive nails deep in His hands,
You thrust the spear within His side.

JOHN RICHARD MORELAND

### Contemporary

Then to "Emmaus" with him I, too, walked.
No mark of nails in hands or feet I traced.
So quietly of star-wise dream he talked,
I did not know a Saviour with me paced
The dripping city street; that by my side,
In the familiar clothes of modern men,
There was rehearsed the tale of One who died
"To make earth good"; the thorns, the scourge again.

At lunch he told in simple phrase to me
The story of the strike and his arrest
Charged with inciting murder. A near tree
Bent while he talked of prison, Death for guest.
And when he spoke of rising from that tomb,
A cross of shadows slanted on the room.

SARA BARD FIELD

### So Runs Our Song

*We admire saints,*
*but insist on our present*
*life*

A dozen sandaled saints I see
Walk the sad soil of Galilee.

Right loud I laud the humble land,
    And the holy crop she grew.
Yet how I love my leech-fed Rome—
    Her tubs and temples, too.
I'd die the death before I'd be
A sandaled saint of Galilee.

So runs our song. And you and I
The Shining One still crucify,
Spit in his face, and pass him by.

MARY EVA KITCHEL

### Tale of One Hill

*X Caesar's Empire*
*dead*

Time erodes the hills?
Not all hills, no, not all.

There was once a little hill
With a tiny speck of a cross on top;
And Caesar laughed—uproariously!—about it:
"A king was he?
Ho! Long live the king!"

But Caesar's Rome decayed and fell;
And when the dust of tumbled glory cleared,   *good.*
The rubble of disintegrated empire had simply
Added stature to the hill.

*Cross towers o'er the*
*wrecks of time.*

It happened again . . .
And again . . .
And again . . .
And even now the air is full of dust
And rumbling, tumbling, cataclysmic sounds.

The hill will be a trifle larger
Tomorrow,
And the cross a little higher! *"If I be lifted up . ."*

FRANKLIN D. ELMER, JR.


## The Cross

Talk not of Justice and her scales of woe; *of Psalm wicked prosp*
We know no justice, weighing gain and loss,
Save the balancing arms of love held wide
That cannot sway or falter to and fro,
Mercy on this side and the other side,
The adamantine justice of the Cross.

*Love does not fluctuate as justice does*

EVA GORE-BOOTH


## Injustice

I heard the verdict, stern and grim—
    And a sigh of God amidst the row.
The powers decreed the cross for Him—
    They are not called Sanhedrins now.

*Act 4*

SHELDON SHEPARD

## Crucifix

Pitted and pock-marked by a roving gun,
The battered image of the Only Son
Stands in the path of war, as a closed gate—
New is the weapon, very old the hate.
Old the derision, old the mercy too,
Crying, "Forgive, they know not what they do."

EDITH LOVEJOY PIERCE

*A crucifix in war.*

## Thought on a News Item

To think that where young Jesus lay,
Whose love has colored our human way,
There should be terror and stratagem.
"A bomb has fallen in Bethlehem."

LUCIA TRENT

## What Would He Say?

What would he say should he come once more,
And saw a shuddering planet burn and bleed?
What would he say, to watch ensanguined greed
Crouch like a spider, sprawled at many a door?
What would he say, to split the blazing core
Of matter, and produce but dragon's seed?
While snarl-and-bicker is the nations' creed,
And chattering terror skulks on every shore?

*atoms devil's fruit*

*Jesus pleads for love. We kill Him*

As though in dream, I hear a soul-deep plea
That throbs and murmurs from a measureless source.
I view a figure preaching; and I see
The crowds that form in raillery or remorse.
And then I mark a crimsoned, nail-pierced tree,
And a torn sufferer moaning on a cross.

STANTON A. COBLENTZ

### Jesus of Nazareth

Would you see the marks of the Roman scourge,
And the pits where the nails were driven?
They are all hidden under fresh wounds.

Much more than forty lashes have I borne since Calvary;
Blows aimed at striking labor have bruised my body sore;
I've known the torture of my kinsmen by the gentile mob;
My back is raw from lashings by heroes, masked, at night.
Wherever man was beaten, I was whipped.

You see this scar?
    'Twas a bayonet in Flanders.
You see this bruise?
    A slave's chain pinched me there.
My shoulders stoop?
    Under the heavy load of labor.

You would see the marks of the Roman scourge,
And the pits where the nails were driven?
They are all hidden under fresh wounds.

ERNEST CADMAN COLWELL

### Crucifixion  WAR

Golgotha's journey is an ancient way
  That leads from Rome's outrageous judgment gate
To modern slums and trenches, where we pray
  To him whose heart is breaking with our hate.

We build his crosses now of steel and lead,
  And pierce his body with the bayonet;
Behind the trenches watch his blood flow red
  In flaming anguish that we soon forget.

Lord Caesar's high tribunal, Martian-wise,
  Spits in his face—Rome never was more rude!—
And in the name of freedom still denies
  To Christian men the right of rectitude.

For greed and self-enthronement are the same,
  And Jesus bleeds in every clan and clime;
All down the ages with its lashing shame
  He bears the insult—Love his only crime.

HUGH O. ISBELL

### New Crucifixion

He arose from the dead,
But again he is crucified;
Wherever an army camps,
Planning for war—
There Jesus again has died,
The glory has fled.

He arose—a new birth—
And the gladness reached heaven's gate,
Earth thrilled to a greater spring;
But alas! since then
The centuries reek with hate,
The war lords rule earth.

He arose—death was slain;
But men would not have it so.
They spurned him, took up the sword,
Set up a cross. . . .
And there, through a night of woe,
Again cries our Lord.

                              THOMAS CURTIS CLARK

### Mother's Petition, in Wartime

Mary Mother, Heart Sublime,
Now we know what anguish thine
As they led your Son away
Treating him as common clay;
Now we know how deep thy cry
As they raised him up to die.

Mary Mother, join the hands
Of the mothers in all lands
In a universal prayer
Of forgiveness, not despair:
"Father, forgive them, all anew,
For they know not what they do."

                              HELEN M. BURGESS

### To Mary, Mother of Christ

I, being Protestant, can never bow
The knee to you, sweet mother of our Lord,
And yet I am a woman and I know
The same bewilderment and fears,
The same necessity for secret tears
That sore beset you. Now
I, being Protestant, can only stand
Here by your side and touch your woman's hand
Across the centuries that intervene,
The tides of peace and war that flow between
Your day and mine; can seek in our accord
Your seal of woman's courage on my brow,
Knowing that when your firstborn died
Upon his cross you too were crucified.

UNA W. HARSEN

### Symbol of Hope

"Among the few things
I brought with me
Is a silver cross
From your uniform
Of the First World War..."
The soldier's letter ran on,
But I paused in thought
While tears filled my eyes;

For he was but a lad
When I took the cross
From my faded coat
And gave it to him.

Among the few things—
That is all the world has:
A Cross on a Hill.

CARL S. WEIST

## The Cross

I saw it in a shell-torn town,
　　A cross, the symbol of his love,
Who left his throne and left his crown
　　And all the loveliness thereof.

Surprised that such an austere thing—
　　So white it shamed the very snow—
Should gleam amid war's trafficking,
　　A sign to solace pain and woe.

A soldier, schooled to challenge love,
　　There at love's shrine I knelt to pray,
For peace and for the gifts thereof . . .
　　The tender kiss at end of day.

DONALD EARL EDWARDS

## New Crucifixion

Now, around the world, the mills
　　Are making spikes that men
May take the Christ, the Lord of Love,
　　To crucify again.

Now the mills are making spears
　　To pierce the Saviour's side;
For men will mock the Son of Man
　　After he has died.

But naught that men can make or do
　　Will hold him in the tomb,
For he will rise eternally
　　To save them from their doom!
　　　　　　EARL BIGELOW BROWN

## The Way

Pass not too near these outcast sons of men
Where walked your Christ ahead! lest you, too, share
The rabble's wrath! in time take heed! beware
The woe—the bitter shame of him again!
Your flaming zeal speak not so rash—so loud!
Keep on your prudent way within the crowd!

What if they mark you of his band, and cry:
"Behold this one, as well!" ah, you should know
The jeers, the stones, for all that with him go!

Have caution, fool! let others yearn and die;
These broken ones you love with hot heartbreak
Can save you not! Be warned by his mistake.
Remember how he spurned the risk and loss!
Remember how they nailed him to a cross!

LAURA SIMMONS

## In a Troubled World

Vainly we crave for some divine Redeemer,
  Not knowing One who beats with bleeding wings
At doors when Man the Sage and Man the Dreamer
  Were driven by the reign of Force and Things.

STANTON A. COBLENTZ

*no salvation for modern man — beco*
*He doesnt know the One (Xst)*

## All Too Slowly

Like a glacier man advances.
  All too slowly does he learn,
Fighting once with spears and lances,
  Now with bombs that blast and burn.

Must he keep forever trying
  To annihilate the race?
Must he keep on crucifying
  Christ in field and market place?

All too slowly, like a glacier
  Man goes on through fog and hate.
May he find the one, the holy
  Way of love before too late!

LUCIA TRENT

## The Jew to Jesus

*[handwritten: X Jews thru the Centuries have been crucified]*

O Man of my own people, I alone
Among these alien ones can know thy face,
I who have felt the kinship of our race
Burn in me as I sit where they intone
Thy praises,—those who, striving to make known
A God for sacrifice, have missed the grace
Of thy sweet human meaning in its place,   *[handwritten: Jesus as man.]*
Thou who art of our blood-bond and our own.

*[handwritten: for men]*

Are we not sharers of thy Passion? Yea,
In spirit-anguish closely by thy side
We have drained the bitter cup, and, tortured, felt
With thee the bruising of each heavy welt.
In every land is our Gethsemane.
A thousand times have we been crucified.

FLORENCE KIPER FRANK

### Golgotha's Cross

What is the cross on Golgotha to me—
But the brave young Jesus murdered there?
Roman justice debased?
Israel's Messiah lost?

The tender lips agonized?
The active mind bewildered?
The feet, that walked fair Galilee,
Pierced by nails?

I have tried to speak
The words those lips revealed.
I have tried to think as he thought.
I have taught my feet to walk
Humbly as he walked.

*And God prepared me a cross.*

The arms reach out to gather in
The cripples, the blind, the weak.
The arms reach out to feed them,
To give them to drink.
In these hands the nails are driven.

But the cross points upward.
The arms fold me.
The cross lifts me.
Golgotha's cross is the road to heaven.

                     RAYMOND KRESENSKY

### It Is Not Finished, Lord

It is not finished, Lord.
There is not one thing done.
There is no battle of my life
That I have really won.
And now I come to tell Thee
How I fought to fail.
I cannot read the writing of the years;
My eyes are full of tears.
It gets all blurred and won't make sense.
It's full of contradictions
Like the scribblings of a child.
I can but hand it in, and hope
That Thy great mind, which reads
The writings of so many lives,
Will understand this scrawl
And what it strives
To say—but leaves unsaid.
I cannot write it over.
The stars are coming out.
My body needs its bed.
I have no strength for more,
So it must stand or fall, dear Lord!—
That's all.

G. A. STUDDERT-KENNEDY

## If He Should Come

If he should come tomorrow, the Meek and Lowly One,
To walk familiar pathways beneath an older sun,
What king would hail his coming, what seer proclaim his
     birth,
If he should come tomorrow, would he find faith on earth?

If he should come tomorrow, what marvels would he see?
White wings that soar the heavens, great ships that sail
     the sea,
A million spires arising to praise his holy name,
But human hearts unchastened, and human greed the same.

As in the days of Herod, the money-changers still
In God's own House contriving against the Father's will;
His messengers in exile, corruption on the throne,
And all the little company disbanded and alone.

Oh, let him come in glory with all the powers of God,
Begirt with shining legions to rule with iron rod,
Till greed be purged forever from out the souls of men;
Lest he who comes tomorrow be crucified again!

LILITH LORRAINE

### From "The Terrible Meek"

Already our kingdoms are beginning to totter.
Possess the earth?
Why, we have lost it! We never did possess it!
We have lost both the earth and our own souls
In trying to possess it!
For the soul of the earth is man and the love of man,
And of them both we have made a despair and a desolation!

I tell you, my good woman, this dead son of yours,
Disfigured, shamed, spat upon,
Has built a kingdom this day that shall never die.
The living glory of him will forever rule it.
The earth is his and he made it.
He and his brothers have been molding and making it
Through all the long ages.
They are the only ones
Who ever really can possess it.
Not the proud, not the idle, not the wealthy,
Not the vaunted empires of this world. . . . No!
Something has happened here upon this hill today,
Something that will shake all the empires and kingdoms
Of this world into the dust.
The earth is his, the earth is theirs, and they made it!
The meek, the terrible meek,
The fierce, agonizing meek,
Are about to come into their inheritance!

CHARLES RANN KENNEDY

### In the Storm

Sometimes I see, against a storm-whipped sky,
Beaten by squalls that lunge in rain and hail,
A pine that twists and writhes beneath the gale,
Like some great soul the ages crucify.
I watch it threshing as the blasts flap by,
Winged with destruction that may soon prevail.
But at day's end, upon the scarred rock-trail,
It stands like truth, still noble-limbed and high.

And in that persecuted tree it seems
I look on one who struggles all unknown,
With bleeding brow, and anguish-darkened face—
A Christ whose spirit conquers and redeems,
Straining upon a windy crest alone,
Pierced by a thorn, to save a suffering race.

STANTON A. COBLENTZ

*beautiful vivid*

# Resurrection

# Resurrection

### Easter Morning

Gray clouds against a leaden sky, *early morning*
  Unlit by any glow of dawn.
Two weeping women hasten by
  Whose love still lives though hope is gone.

The day breaks dull and red without
  A cheering ray for those who grieve.
Two men come running who dare not doubt
  The thing they dare not yet believe.

The tomb is open. He lives! He lives!
  Death is dead and night is done.
Earth shouts with joy, and heaven gives
  Its gift of gold in the risen sun.

197

Again the darkness closes in
    Upon a world grown cold and wise,
With gloom of greed, and murk of sin,
    When men forget his shining eyes.

Roll back the clouds of hate, and fling
    Apart the curtains of the night.
In hearts that love and souls that sing
    Let Christ arise. Let there be light!

WINFRED ERNEST GARRISON

### Resurrection

*lovely*

It came so quietly—the first gray light,
That touched the open tomb that Easter dawn,
Long years ago. There, where the weight of night
And death had lain a dark despair upon
Each sorrowing heart, came morning, a bird's voice,
And cypress trees showed sunrise trickling through.
The day that bade the whole wide world rejoice
Was born where lilies in a garden grew.

It will come quietly. There will be bread,
Water for long-parched lips. The hurt-filled breast
Will sense a healing comfort, void of dread.
Slowly earth's war-torn peoples will have rest
And, with its life, its light, its sweet release,
Like that first Easter morning, will come peace.

IDA NORTON MUNSON

*Could be a prayer*

## My Saviour

My Saviour in Gethsemane
  Knelt anguished and alone,
And pledged his unreluctant faith:
  "Thy will, not mine, be done."

My Saviour, dying on the cross—
  A humbled, hated Jew—
With deep compassion prayed, "Forgive!
  They know not what they do."

My Saviour, risen from the tomb,
  Spoke words that bring release,
His final testament of love:
  "I give to you My peace."

MARY HALLET

## Easter

With song and sun-burst comes the Easter morn:
Yet was there sunset ere the sun arose;
Under the sod, the rain-drift and the snows,
The nurturing of life, wherefrom was born
The blossom on the breast of beauty worn.
Each way of glory through some garden goes
Where midnight yet a deeper midnight knows,
Against the halo, cross and scourge and thorn.
Will it be always so? the Easter still

Always the answer to what seemeth ill?
Or shall we some day know that all is good
If but the all, at last, be understood?
This the consummate Easter that shall be
In the full sun-burst of Eternity!

ROBERT WHITAKER

## Easter Message

Almost two thousand years ago today
The stone upon His grave was rolled away,
And in the blinding darkness of the tomb
He rose and shattered there the grief and gloom
Within the hearts of those who worshiped Him.
Although that day and time have now grown dim,
One message through the ages has been hurled:
His love is hope and light for all the world.
And as the dawn of Easter fills the skies
We, too, with Him in spirit must arise;
For even underneath us in the earth
There is a faithful promise of rebirth.
If there's a stone against your heart today,
Look up to Him and it will roll away.

JOHN VAN BRAKLE

## Hope

*He died!*
And with him perished all that men hold dear;
Hope lay beside him in the sepulcher,
Love grew corse cold, and all things beautiful beside
Died when he died.

*He rose!*
And with him hope arose, and life and light.
Men said, "Not Christ but Death died yesternight."
And joy and truth and all things virtuous
Rose when he rose.

ANONYMOUS

## Easter Night

All night had shout of men and cry
Of woeful women filled his way;
Until that noon of somber sky
On Friday, clamor and display
Smote him; no solitude had he,
No silence, since Gethsemane.

Public was Death; but Power, but Might,
But Life again, but Victory,
Were hushed within the dead of night,
The shuttered dark, the secrecy.
And all alone, alone, alone
He rose again behind the stone.

ALICE MEYNELL

### Dawn

Near the dawn Mary went,
Grief-led, to serve the Dead;
Though the Miracle seemed spent,
Ye stricken know why Mary went.   *You who have gone thru it*

Through the dawn Simon came.
For him, the mock of a distant cock
Coiled anew a lash of flame;
Ye faithless know why Simon came.

Down the dawn angels sped,
Radiant flight out-winging light.
"Christ lives!" they sang. "He that was dead!"
Ye deathless know why angels sped!

MIRIAM LeFevre Crouse

### Mary   *His mother at the grave, thinking; of what? Bethlehem? His birth*

On the first Easter, ere the harbinger
Of that new Dawn its first low note had sung,
While o'er the garden grieving night yet hung
And Mary waited by the sepulcher,
I wonder if the silence held for her
The echo of a courtly Eastern tongue;   *wise men*
If, bearing spikenard, she yet bravely clung
To memory of frankincense and myrrh.
Still did she keep the glory of Bethlehem,

Pondering the marvels at the manger's side,
So in her hour of darkness comforted?
Or did the cross outside Jerusalem,
Where with dimmed eyes she saw him crucified,
Shadow all else but this: "My Son is dead"?

NELLIE KNIGHT

## Mary Knew

Trembling with grief came Mary Magdalene,
Nor heard the birds, nor saw the lilies' sheen
Glow in the early morning drip of dew;
Nor thought she of the dim light shining through
The gently stirring leaves of cypress trees,
Nor of the fragrant garden—all of these
The things the Master loved. Lonely she wept.
Then quietly, not to disturb, she crept
Where she could see the great stone rolled away—
Angels where she had thought his body lay.
Softly she asked: "Where have they laid my Lord?" . . .
She must believe the angels' awesome word
That he had risen. How could she doubt? And yet
She lingered near the tomb and still she wept.

"Mary!" Her name. And then she saw his face.
Her Lord! *Alive.* Without one single trace
Of doubt, her joy has braved the centuries.
The empty tomb, the angel messages—
From these her stricken heart cold comfort drew . . .
Mary had seen her Lord. She *knew.* She *knew.*

IDA NORTON MUNSON

## As It Began to Dawn

A sound, a sigh; a whip of rushing air.
A dazzling sky wheeled back, rolled down: below,
Thunders withdrawn behind the lightning glare
Rattle Death's kettledrums with rumbling woe.
Dawn cracks: Heaven crumbles. In a swift travail
Earth heaves vast-mountained shoulders, draws new breath.
The stars wheel glittering from the trackless trail
To thrust their pointed fires at dying Death.
The tomb, still-shaken, works in paling night,
Shatters with a brazen trumpet sigh,
As from the East the glad ecstatic light
Showers Creation with a burning cry:
*He lives! From Death's long uncontested place*
*The Son of God comes forth in regal grace.*

GEORGE EDWARD HOFFMAN

## The Hour Is Late

The hour is late. Slow, slow our steps have been.
Mary has long since sped upon her way—
The thorns, the cross, the tomb, all held within
Her grieving heart. Yet, now, on this third day,
The memory of Christ's deep trust in her
Has winged her feet. In spite of fear, alone,
Spices held close, she seeks the sepulcher,
To find someone has rolled away the stone.

The hour is late. Disciples, too, have sought
The place in which his precious flesh was laid;
And, "He Is Risen," words the angels brought,
Have voiced their comforting for hearts afraid.
Speed, speed our steps! For still the lilies bloom,
And glows the garden with its empty tomb.

IDA NORTON MUNSON

## Easter

Lord, now that Spring is in the world,
  And every tulip is a cup
Filled with the wine of Thy great love,
  Lift Thou me up.

Raise Thou my heart as flowers arise
  To greet the glory of Thy day,
With soul as clean as lilies are,
  And white as they.

Let me not fear the darkness now,
  Since Life and Light break through Thy tomb;
Teach me that doubts no more oppress,
  No more consume.

Show me that Thou art April, Lord,
  And Thou the flowers and the grass;
Then, when awake the soft spring winds,
  I'll hear Thee pass!

CHARLES HANSON TOWNE

## Mary Magdalene

At dawn she sought the Saviour slain,
To kiss the spot where he had lain
And weep warm tears, like springtime rain;

When lo, there stood, unstained of death,
A man that spoke with low sweet breath;
And "Master!" Mary answereth.

From out the far and fragrant years
How sweeter than the songs of seers
That tender offering of tears!

RICHARD BURTON

*true; the love of Mary for her Lord.*

*good contrast X*

## Tombs

Egyptian tombs hold priceless things,
Scepters and crowns and rings,
And ornaments of cunning skill
To humor the imperial will
Of mummied potentates.
Full tombs,
Great corridors and rooms,
To tell of ancient powers and high estates.

And has an empty tomb no glory shed?
"He is not here; he is risen," the angel said.

LOUISE WEBSTER

### The Garden

The garden now is sealed and dead,
But, lo! a crocus lifts its head;
This is the tomb of Love, we feel,
But here an iris breaks the seal.
This is not death but wonted birth,
But resurrection of the frost-bound earth;
The silver rain unseals the crust
And through the sod green spears will thrust
Returning spring, renew our faith,
For he is risen as he saith.

BELLE F. OWENS

### He Is Risen

The Lord indeed is risen
From out his earthly prison,
And now, all kings above,
He reigns forevermore—
The Lord of Life, the King of Love,
Life's loving Conqueror.

JOHN OXENHAM

### From "Christmas Eve"

Earth breaks up, time drops away,
In flows heaven, with its new day
Of endless life, when he who trod,

Very Man and Very God,
This Earth in weakness, shame and pain,
Dying the death whose signs remain
Up yonder on the accursèd tree—
Shall come again, no more to be
Of Captivity the thrall,
But the One God, all in all,
King of Kings and Lord of Lords,
As his servant John received the words,
"I died, and live forevermore!"

ROBERT BROWNING

## Resurrection and Ascension

He built a kingdom with his heart and brain,
He knew hosannas and the psalms, till one
Played Judas for a paltry little gain,
And in that hour his kingdom was undone.
His spirit entering Gethsemane,
Enduring bitter, bitter hours alone,
At last went staggering to Calvary,
From thence to hell—and found a bed of stone.

But when the lilies flamed he breathed again,
A man of scars, yet luminous and strange
With ecstasy unknown to other men—
An ecstasy no Judas kiss may change.
The hosts who fled now worship from afar:
They kneel before the beauty of a star.

EARL D. TODD

### Easter Carol

O Earth! throughout thy borders
  Re-don thy fairest dress;
And everywhere, O Nature,
  Throb with new happiness;
Once more to new creation
  Awake, and death gainsay,
For death is swallowed up of life,
  And Christ is risen today.

Let peals of jubilation
  Ring out in all the lands;
With hearts of deep elation
  Let sea with sea clasp hands;
Let one supreme Te Deum
  Roll round the world's highway,
For death is swallowed up of life,
  And Christ is risen today.
          GEORGE NEWELL LOVEJOY

### Easter Music

Blow, golden trumpets, sweet and clear,
Blow soft upon the perfumed air;
Bid the sad earth to join our song,
*"To Christ does victory belong!"*

Oh, let the winds your message bear
To every heart of grief and care;
Sound through the world the joyful lay,
*"Our Christ hath conquered Death today!"*

On cloudy wings let glad words fly
Through the soft blue of echoing sky:
Ring out, O trumpets, sweet and clear,
*"Through Death immortal Life is here!"*

MARGARET WADE DELAND

### From "Easter Hymn"
#### (*In "Faust"*)

Christ is arisen,
    Joy to thee, mortal!
Out of his prison,
    Forth from its portal!
Christ is not sleeping,
    Seek him no longer;
Strong was his keeping,
    Jesus was stronger.

Christ is arisen,
    Seek him not here;
Lonely his prison,
    Empty his bier;
Vain his entombing,
    Spices and lawn,
Vain the perfuming,
    Jesus is gone.

Christ is arisen,
  Joy to thee, mortal!
Empty his prison,
  Broken his portal!
Rising, he giveth
  His shroud to the sod;
Risen, he liveth,
  And liveth to God.

                    J. W. von Goethe


## Resurrection — *His resurrection was mine too, — my real self enbured*

I did not know, the day I nailed
  The Christ upon a tree,
That he whom I despised and railed
  Had been the better me.                    X

I never dreamed, the day I sealed
  His love within a tomb,
That I had willfully congealed
  My nobler self in gloom.

But when the stone was rolled away
  (Who loves can never die),
There was no doubt that Easter Day:
  The one who rose was I.

                    Lloyd Frank Merrell

## Easter Joy

I, too, O Christ, denied you,
　　And felt the dawn-winds blow
Cold and gray upon my cheek,
　　And heard the cock's loud crow;

I, too, sat silent while the scribes
　　With cynic wisdom tried,
Buffeted, reviled and mocked,
　　Condemned you—crucified.

But I have seen the dead arise,
　　The spring wake fair and strong;
And doubt has changed to soaring faith,
　　Despair to love and song.

DAISY CONWAY PRICE

## An Easter Canticle

In every trembling bud and bloom
　　That cleaves the earth, a flowery sword,
I see Thee come from out the tomb,
　　Thou risen Lord.

In every April wind that sings
　　Down lanes that make the heart rejoice,
Yea, in the word the woodthrush brings,
　　I hear Thy voice.

Lo, every tulip is a cup
   To hold Thy morning's brimming wine.
Drink, O my soul, the wonder up—
   Is it not Thine?

The great Lord God, invisible,
   Hath roused to rapture the green grass;
Through sunlit mead and dew-drenched dell
   I see him pass.

His old immortal glory wakes
   The rushing streams and emerald hills;
His ancient trumpet softly shakes
   The daffodils.

Thou art not dead! Thou art the whole
   Of life that quickens in the sod.
Green April is Thy very soul,            *naturalism*
   Thou great Lord God.
                          CHARLES HANSON TOWNE

## The Stone

"Christ is risen, Christ is risen!"
   The glad voices glibly say,              *unmoved—
Yet he lies within the prison              sed-groomed.*
   Of our stolid hearts today.

No angel rolls away the stone
   Of cowardice and greed.
It is our strength and ours alone
   Can answer for that need.

Grant us strength in straining, lifting,
   He on his side, we on ours,
Till at length, the boulder shifting,
   Christ comes forth among the flowers.

KENNETH W. PORTER

## Echoes of Jesus

A little inn in Bethlehem first heard the echo of his voice,
His footsteps on sands of Galilee aroused the ocean to
   rejoice,
And on the road to Calvary his gospel sounded near and
   far
Like a reflected glory on the Cross of one great Star.

His gentle hands were joined with native wood cut from
   his native trees
That echoed with the ax and hammer of his earthly
   enemies.
His body whispered sorrow in leaf of flesh, in branch of
   bone,
But, oh, what strength sang from the soul that rolled away
   the stone!

LUCILE COLEMAN

## "If a Man Die, Shall He Live Again?"

I will repudiate the lie
Men tell of life;
How it will pass
As fragile flower, or butterfly,
Whose dust shall nourish
April grass.

Since One, for love, died on a tree
And in the stony
Tomb was lain,
Behold I show a mystery:
All sepulchres
Are sealed in vain!

JOHN RICHARD MORELAND


### A Song at Easter

If this bright lily
    Can live once more,
And its white promise
    Be as before,
Why cannot the great stone
    Be moved from his door?

If the green grass
    Ascend and shake
Year after year,

And blossoms break
Again and again
    For April's sake,

Why cannot he,
    From the dark and mold,
Show us again
    His manifold
And gleaming glory,
    A stream of gold?

Faint heart, be sure
    These things must be.
See the new bud
    On the old tree! . . .
If flowers can wake,
    Oh, why not He?
                CHARLES HANSON TOWNE


## Resurrection

In this brown seed, so dry and hard,
I see a flower in my door yard.
You, chrysalis in winding sheet,
Are butterfly all dainty sweet.
All life is warmed by spring's sweet breath,
And Christ our Lord has conquered death.
                AGNES W. STORER

### Easter

Today unnumbered church bells ring.
　　Unnumbered hands are clasped in prayer
To Him who suffered, lived, and died,
　　And rose from sorrow and despair.

This is the season for rebirth
　　Of human hope and joy and love,
When beauty blooms again on earth
　　And brighter glows the sky above.

The cold things in this changing world
　　Have no place in your heart today,
For even Winter's icy shroud
　　Has long since thawed and flowed away.

So listen as the church bells ring
　　And clasp your hands again in prayer,
Then joyfully arise and sing;
　　His love will conquer your despair.

JOHN VAN BRAKLE

### Christ Has Risen

Christ has risen—else in vain
All the sunshine, all the rain,
All the warmth and quickening,
And renewal of the spring.
Vain they were to charm our eyes,

Greening earth and gracious skies,
Growth and beauty, bud or bloom,
If within their fast-sealed tomb
All our dearer dead must dwell,
Sharing not the miracle.

Crocus tips in shining row,
Welcome, for your sign we know.
Every bud on every bough
Has its message for us now,
Since the Lord on Easter Day
Burst the bonds of prisoning clay;
All the springtime has a voice,
Every heart may dare rejoice,
Every grave, no more a prison,
Joins the chorus, "Christ is risen."

SUSAN COOLIDGE

### Easter Light

Because upon the first glad Easter day
The stone that sealed his tomb was rolled away,
So, through the deepening shadows of death's night,
Men see an open door—beyond it, light.

IDA NORTON MUNSON

## Resurrection

If it be all for nought, for nothingness
At last, why does God make the world so fair?
Why spill this golden splendor out across
The western hills, and light the silver lamp
Of eve? Why give me eyes to see, the soul
To love so strong and deep? Then, with a pang
This brightness stabs me through, and wakes within
Rebellious voice to cry against all death?
Why set this hunger for eternity
To gnaw my heartstrings through, if death ends all?
If death ends all, then evil must be good,
Wrong must be right, and beauty ugliness.
God is a Judas who betrays his Son
And, with a kiss, damns all the world to hell—
If Christ rose not again.

UNKNOWN SOLDIER, *killed in World War I*


## The Road to Emmaus

Twilight. And on a dusty ribboned way,
Out from Jerusalem, two travelers walked.
Gray shadows touched their feet, but deeper lay
The shadows in their hearts. They softly talked
Of days just passed, of hopeless days in view,
Of boats, of nets, the while their eyes were dim,
Of Galilee, the work they used to do;
Their voices often stilled, remembering him.

A stranger also walked that way, and when
They sensed his nearness, some new sympathy
Assuaged their grief. Old hopes came warm again
As, in the dusk, he kept them company. . . .
Thus, through the troubled twilight of today
Emmaus road has stretched its shining thread
And still Christ walks beside men on the way,
To hold the light of hope, to break the bread.

IDA NORTON MUNSON

## The Sepulcher in the Garden

What though the Flowers in Joseph's Garden grew
Of rarest perfume and of fairest hue,
That morn when Magdalene hastened through
   Its fragrant, silent paths?

She caught no scent of budding almond tree;
Her eyes, tear-blinded still from Calvary,
Saw neither lily nor anemone—
   Naught save the Sepulcher.

But when the Master whispered "Mary," lo!
The Tomb was hid; the Garden all ablow;
And burst in bloom the Rose of Jericho—
   From that day "Mary's Flower."

JOHN FINLEY

## They Saw and Believed

*a beautiful poem*
*to narrate that*
*3rd morning*

And after Calvary, a garden, green
With spring. Cool lilies lent their healing hush,
And surely from some blossoming bough a thrush
Fluted a sundown lullaby, unseen.
Within the garden was a tomb, hand-hewn
From rock, and there friends laid his body; wound
About him linen fine and white, and bound
In myrrh and aloes. Then they rolled a stone
Against the door. . . . Before a second dawn
The sorrowing Marys found an open tomb,
With glistening angels lighting up the gloom—
"Jesus is risen! Come, see that he is gone!"
Amazed disciples enter there to grieve—
They see the linen clothes, and they believe!

ESTHER LLOYD HAGG


## Incense

Fragrance drifts through our thoughts of Him:
Frankincense and myrrh . . .
The scent of vineyards on sun-warmed hills
And fields where lilies stir . . .
Dawn, and a garden, dew-sweet, that held
An empty sepulcher.

LESLIE SAVAGE CLARK

# Come, Follow Me

# Come, Follow Me

## What Is It Jesus Saith?

What is it Jesus saith unto the soul?
"Take up the cross, and come and follow Me."
One word he saith to all men: none may be
Without a cross yet hope to reach the goal.
Then heave it bravely up, and brace thy whole
Body to bear: it will not weigh on thee
Past strength; or if it crush thee to thy knee
Take heart of grace, for grave shall be thy dole.

Give thanks today, and let tomorrow take
Heed to itself; today imports thee more.
Tomorrow may not dawn like yesterday:
Until that unknown tomorrow go thy way,
Suffer and work and strive for Jesus' sake—
Who tells thee what tomorrow keeps in store?

Christina G. Rossetti

225

*Good on creedal controversy*

## "Come, Follow Me!"

Athwart the jangling of our creeds is heard,
From out the past, one calm, clear word;
A Son of Wisdom walked beside the sea,
And said unto his friends, "Come, follow me."

And they who rose and followed left behind
Their small disputes. Slow yielding to his mind,
They found a master purpose. He was King,
Whose love had lured them from their trafficking.

*But we must not forget doctrine*

How foolish we who set against an age
Distraught and lost our creedal heritage!
There stands a world of hate, of vision dim:
That we might speak the words, "Come, follow him!"

THOMAS CURTIS CLARK

## The Better Part

Long fed on boundless hopes, O race of man,
How angrily thou spurn'st all simpler fare!
"Christ," some one says, "was human as we are;
No judge eyes us from heaven, our sin to scan;
We live no more, when we have done our span."—
"Well, then, for Christ," thou answerest, "who can care?
From sin, which Heaven records not, why forbear?
Live we like brutes our life without a plan!"

So answerest thou; but why not rather say:
"Hath man no second life?"—*Pitch this one high!*
Sits there no judge in Heaven, our sin to see?—
"*More strictly, then, the inward judge obey!* Conscience
Was Christ a man like us? *Ah, let us try*
*If we then, too, can be such men as he!*"

MATTHEW ARNOLD

## Eucharist    X good.

Still we who follow Christ in deed
    Must break the bread and spill the wine:
Still must a costly Eucharist
    Be for a sacrifice and sign.

Our bodies broken for the truth
    By mobs or Pharisees of State
Must be the bread which Liberty
    Feeds on, and lives, and waxes great.

Our blood, our covenant of love,
    Is the rich wine which we must give
To a sick world that hates the gift—
    So, by our dying, God may live.

Not by the grape or wheaten bread
    Can we partake the Eucharist:
Communion is to give to God
    Our blood and bodies, like the Christ.

E. MERRILL ROOT

*Our sacrament is self-sacrifice for God & country.*

## "Love Suffereth Long"

The Writ of Loving Well
     Still makes its old demands:
A sometime residence in Hell,
     The nailprints in the hands.

All those who pledge themselves,
     And to its terms agree,
Must chance an unexclusive cross,
     A common Calvary!
               SARA HENDERSON HAY

## Sacrament

There lies no magic in this bit of bread,
     No charm to save me in this sip of wine.
No food can nourish if the soul be dead,
     No lifeless heart respond to fire divine.

Here at God's altar I may kneel in vain
     Unless I glow with love, selfless and deep.
When I do truly serve my fellow men
     The Eucharist I keep.
               UNA W. HARSEN

## Communion

*[handwritten: good on fellowship]*

I would be one with Thee.
*And is thy brother near?*
He would not come with me.
*Go thou, and bring him here.*
And if he does not come?
*Then come not thou to me;*
*We must be Three in One,*
*Thyself and he in Me.*

LOREN W. BURCH

*[handwritten in right margin: Don't come to God unless you're forgiven your transgressers — Lord's prayer]*

*[handwritten in left margin: Another trinity God - man - man]*

## Imitation of Christ

Taking your life as one long Eucharist
Did you but see yourself
A figure, bent in consecration,
Before a crucifix?
Waiting for some blind world
To bid you walk with holy step
A Via Dolorosa?
Or, more simply, having seen your Risen Christ,
Assumed that you had but one task,
To die another holy death
Against a torn night sky?

Blind soul and egoist!
Break you your daily bread
In sacrament and simplicity;
Pour out your wine and let it be
Communion and rebirth.

WILMA C. LUDLOW

### "If Any Man Would Come After Me"

Be anxious if Christ presses on your life
　As light as dust upon a moth's dull wing;
His word a cross is, his will a strife
　Nor borne nor won by easy following.

He crushed dissemblers with a quiet glance;
　He smashed a nation with a metaphor;
But ah, the pain was not a circumstance
　To his swift healing when the hurt was sore.

EDWIN McNEILL POTEAT

### Follow Me

Lord, I would follow, but—
First, I would see what means that wondrous call
That peals so sweetly through Life's rainbow hall,
That thrills my heart with quivering golden chords,
And fills my soul with joys seraphical.

Lord, I would follow, but—
First, I would leave things straight before I go,—
Collect my dues, and pay the debts I owe;
Lest when I'm gone, and none is here to tend,
Time's ruthless hand my garnering o'erthrow.

Lord, I would follow, but—
First, I would see the end of this high road
That stretches straight before me, fair and broad;
So clear the way I cannot go astray,
It surely leads me equally to God.

Lord, I would follow,—yea,
Follow I *will*,—but first so much there is
That claims me in life's vast emergencies,—
Wrongs to be righted, great things to be done;
Shall I neglect these vital urgencies?

*Who answers Christ's insistent call*
*Must give himself, his life, his all,*
*Without one backward look.*
*Who sets his hand unto the plow,*
*And glances back with anxious brow,*
*His calling hath mistook.*
*Christ claims him wholly for his own;*
*He must be Christ's, and Christ's alone.*

JOHN OXENHAM

## Disillusioned

Through years our minds have wrestled—and how vain!—
With age-old doctrines, born of argument.
The years have left us bitter, spirit-spent.
For our stupendous toil, how little gain!
The Holy Word, which came to guide our way,
Has been an anvil for our mighty thought!
Its living truth, by suffering prophets bought,
Has long been lost amid the critics' fray.

How foolish we! O Man of Nazareth,
Who talked with peasants of the lily's charm,
Who took the little child upon your arm,
Return and save us, Master, from this death.
Speak to our hearts, as once by Galilee,
And bid us, heavy-laden, follow Thee.

THOMAS CURTIS CLARK

## What Christ Said

I said, "Let me walk in the fields."
    He said, "No; walk in the town."
I said, "There are no flowers there."
    He said, "No flowers, but a crown."

I said, "But the skies are black,
    There is nothing but noise and din";
And he wept as he sent me back;
    "There is more," he said, "there is sin."

I said, "But the air is thick,
    And fogs are veiling the sun."
He answered, "Yet souls are sick,
    And souls in the dark undone."

I said, "I shall miss the light,
    And friends will miss me, they say."
He answered, "Choose tonight
    If I am to miss you, or they."

I pleaded for time to be given.
    He said, "Is it hard to decide?
It will not seem hard in Heaven
    To have followed the steps of your Guide."

I cast one look at the fields,
    Then set my face to the town;
He said, "My child, do you yield?
    Will you leave the flowers for the crown?"

Then into his hand went mine;
    And into my heart came he;
And I walk in a light divine,
    The path I had feared to see.

GEORGE MACDONALD

## Thy Kingdom Come!

O Christ, great Lover of all souls,
    Meek Lord of sympathy,
Our lips, how eloquent they are!
    Our hearts, how far from Thee!

*denominations*

We worship our dividing walls,
  We boast our caste and clan;
Oh, let Thy Kingdom quickly come—
  A brotherhood of man.

*good X*

If any churchly fashions lurk
  To thwart Thy larger will,
Let them in love be crucified
  As we Thy wish fulfill.

Renew in us "good will to men,"
  Transform our selfish creeds,
That we may pray "Thy Kingdom come"
  In eloquence of deeds.

THOMAS CURTIS CLARK

*Serve Thy kingdom — do the thing well !*

### Soul-feeding Hyacinths        X

Be with us, Lord, today,
And set us free
From foolish bickerings,
From cant and pettiness, the ugly things
That keep us less
Than Thou wouldst have us be;
Open our eyes that we may see
The Vision Beautiful,
And if we are enmeshed
In dreary labyrinths of everyday,
Grant us release,
And give us peace, O Lord;
An understanding sure and swift,

The very precious gift
Of loving insight. Help us to change
The bread and butter of monotony
Into soul-feeding hyacinths,
Fragrant with service; and until we take
The noblest, highest, truest way,
Let us not rest content;
And of our fellowship today
Help us to make
A joyous sacrament.

*Make us to enjoy the sacrament of Xian fellowship*

CORINNE FARLEY

*excellent* ✗

## A Prayer for Christian Unity   *a prayer.*

O Master of the Galilean Way,
Forgive us for the vows we fail to keep:
Forgive us that we so neglect Thy sheep,
So idly waste this shining harvest day!
Forgive us for the stumblingblocks we lay
Along the paths by which men seek Thee! Sweep
From our small minds the strife that holds Thee cheap! ✗
Break Thou the bread of life with us, we pray!

What matter if we cannot understand
The mystery of Love that is divine,
Nor pierce the veil! Dear Lord, our faith increase
To know that, since our hands may reach Thy hand,
Our lives are made all-powerful, through Thine,
To heal a wounded world and bring it peace!

MOLLY ANDERSON HALEY

### From "Gareth and Lynette"
#### (*In "Idylls of the King"*)

Man am I grown, a man's work must I do.
Follow the deer? follow the Christ, the King,
Live pure, speak true, right wrong, follow the King—
Else, wherefore born?

*[handwritten: why]*

ALFRED TENNYSON

*[handwritten: good.]*

*[handwritten: If we had these things we wooldn't need God. But since we don't, we need Him]*

### Had There Been Peace

Had there been peace on earth, we might have said:
"Without thy presence we are comforted."

Had there been light, we could have said: "Retire.
We are content with lesser, lunar fire."

Had there been beauty, reason, order, law,
We might have cried: "Thou Son of Man, withdraw."

Had there been love, we would have begged: "Depart,
Disturb not Thou the all-sufficient heart."

But there is neither joy nor peace at all
Outside the orbit of Thy tender call.

And if Thou turn Thy pitying face away,
Cold is our life, extinguished is our day.

Abandon not Thy creatures here below.
O Son of God, to whom else shall we go?

EDITH LOVEJOY PIERCE

## Prayer

White Captain of my soul, lead on;
I follow Thee, come dark or dawn.
Only vouchsafe three things I crave:
Where terror stalks, help me be brave!
Where righteous ones can scarce endure
The siren call, help me be pure!
Where vows grow dim, and men dare do
What once they scorned, help me be true!

ROBERT FREEMAN

## The Password

*X Oh yea? Not works, but faith saves*

When I shall come before Thy gate and stand
Knocking for entrance there, if Thou demand
That I should tell my faith, with head bent low,
I needs must answer, "Lord, I do not know,
Save that I held Love best"; to Thy demands
For count of what I did, my empty hands
Must bear sure witness that, of things I wrought,
Worthy the bringing I accomplished naught.

But this is foolishness. I hold no fear
That Thou wilt so demand. I shall draw near
Firm in my tread, and fling the portal wide,
Waiting no invitation. "Lord, I tried"
For all a Password, that my lips shall send
To meet Thine instant answer, "Pass, My friend."

REGINALD C. EVA

### From "Before"

Our wars are wars of life, and wounds of love,
With intellect spears and long-winged arrows of thought,
Mutual, in one another's wrath, all renewing
We live as One Man. For contracting our infinite senses
We behold multitude; or expanding, we behold as One,
As one man all the Universal Family; and that man
We call Jesus the Christ, and he in us, and we in him,
Live in perfect harmony in Eden the land of life,
Giving, receiving, and forgiving each other's trespasses.

ROBERT BROWNING

### Insubordination

"Forgive *yourself*" is part of the command;
The pardon, generous, is incomplete
If half of it I, willful, countermand,
Continuing to grovel at his feet.

MARGARET EVELYN SINGLETON

### Lord Jesus, When We Stand Afar

Lord Jesus, when we stand afar,
   And gaze upon Thy holy cross,
In love of Thee, and scorn of self,
   O may we count the world as loss.

When we behold Thy bleeding wounds,
   And the rough way that Thou hast trod,
Make us to hate the load of sin
   That lay so heavy on our God.

O holy Lord, uplifted high,
   With outstretched arms, in mortal woe,
Embracing in Thy wondrous love
   The sinful world that lies below,

Give us an ever-living faith *Heb 11*
   To gaze beyond the things we see;
And in the mystery of Thy death
   Draw us and all men unto Thee.

WILLIAM WALSHAM HOW

### Miracle

   Oh, paltry miracles
      That satisfy
   The heart: emollient clay
      On blinded eye;

   The mortal foot that walked
      Upon the wave,
   The meager fish and loaf
      Of bread I gave!

   Oh, darkly seeing eyes
      That praise and damn, *The miracle*
   Blind to the miracle: *love*
      I love . . . I am.

EDITH MIRICK

### Fishers in the Night

It was all over now. The populace
Had slain the Master. Stoutly Peter swore,
"I go a-fishing." The two Zebedees
Uncoiled the nets. They pushed off from the shore.

It was all over now: the dusty road,
Beggars and Pharisees, the sick abed,
The sinners' hungry need, His face aflame,
Two healing hands laid on an aching head.

It was all over now. The lake was cool.
Vainly they labored through the night. The sun
Revealed the Master waiting on the sands.
They beached to find that life was but begun.

BEULAH MAY

*How true on conversion — only the beginning.*

### Prayer

Oh, kneel to that God force of love,
To that Christ dream for man,
And know the only power there is
To build the world again!

LUCIA TRENT

*on love*

### Prayer

Thou who didst multiply, by Galilee,
Scant loaves and fishes for humanity,
Teach us to multiply our love and care
Till no least life goes hungering anywhere.

FRANCES CROSBY HAMLET

### Is This Presumption?

Is this presumption, Lord,
to ask
that we be spared the role of slaves to Death,
and that our sacrifices,
even as your own,
may build the road of Life?

LOUISE H. TONESS

### Palm Sunday Hymn

Looking back across the years, O Christ, we see Thee go
'Midst hosannas of the throngs passing to and fro,
'Midst the adoration cries ringing on Thy way—
Voices of the wavering ones lifted for a day.

We hosannas echo on, O Christ, and lift to Thee
Songs of adoration too, and bend adoring knee,
But, though faltering and weak, may we not forget
Like the throngs of long ago, the Heart that loveth yet.

Help us to follow all the way, O Christ, nor turn aside.
'Midst Thy shadows, or Thy light, there would we abide;
Though the world hath scarred Thy name, mark it on our
    breast—
Sweetest name in all the world that ever Love confessed.

GEORGE KLINGLE

## The Good Shepherd

O Shepherd with the bleeding Feet,
Good Shepherd with the pleading Voice,
    What seekest Thou from hill to hill?
Sweet were the valley pastures, sweet
The sound of flocks that bleat their joys,
    And eat and drink at will.
Is one worth seeking, when Thou hast Thine
                    Ninety and nine?

CHRISTINA G. ROSSETTI

# The Continuing Christ

# The Continuing Christ

## The Continuing Christ

*excellent*  X X

Far, far away is Bethlehem,
　　And years are long and dim,
Since Mary held the Holy Child
　　And angels sang for Him.
But still to hearts where love and faith
　　Make room for Christ in them,
He comes again, the Child from God,
　　To find His Bethlehem.

Beyond the sea is Galilee
　　And ways which Jesus trod,
And hidden there are those high hills
　　Where He communed with God;
Yet on the plains of common life,
　　Through all the world of men,

245

The voice that once said, "Follow me,"
    Speaks to our hearts again.

Gethsemane and Calvary
    And death and bitter loss,
Are these but echoes drifting down
    From a forgotten cross?
Nay, Lord, for all our living sins
    Thy cross is lifted up,
And as of old we hear Thee say,
    "Can ye, too, drink My cup?"

O Life that seems so long ago,
    And yet is ever new,
The fellowship of love with Thee,
    Through all the years is true.
O Master over death and time,
    Reveal Thyself, we pray,
And as before amongst Thine own,
    Dwell Thou in us today!

W. Russell Bowie

## The Faith of Christ's Freemen

Our faith is in the Christ who walks
    With men today, in street and mart;
The constant Friend who thinks and talks
    With those who seek him with the heart.

His gospel calls for living men
    With singing blood and minds alert;

Strong men, who fall to rise again,
  Who strive and bleed, with courage girt.

We serve no God whose work is done,
  Who rests within his firmament:
Our God, his labors but begun,
  Toils evermore, with power unspent.

God was and is and e'er shall be;
  Christ lived and loved—and loves us still;
And man goes forward, proud and free,
  God's present purpose to fulfill.

THOMAS CURTIS CLARK

### The White Presence

  Will not our hearts within us burn
    On the darkening road,
  If a White Presence we can discern—
    Despite an ancient load?

  Whither goest Thou, Pilgrim Friend?
    Lone Figure far ahead,
  Wilt Thou not tarry until the end—
    And break our bread?

  Follow we must amid sun or shade,
    Our faith to complete,
  Journeying where no path is made—
    Save by His feet!

JOSEPH FORT NEWTON

*He lives to me*
*∴ I know.*

## Reality

Not from two who supped with You
   At an inn as twilight fell
Do I know that Joseph's tomb
   Was an empty shell.

Not from Peter or from John
   Or from Mary or from Paul
Did I learn how life can change
   At Your call.

Not on the Damascus road
   Or in any far off place
Did my spirit see the dawn
   Of Your face.

Those who lived in Galilee
   Knew their Lord and held him dear—
But my Lord has come to me
   Now and here.

               Amelia Josephine Burr

## Judean Hills Are Holy

Judean hills are holy,
   Judean fields are fair,
For one can find the footprints
   Of Jesus everywhere.

One finds them in the twilight
   Beneath the singing sky,
Where shepherds watched in wonder
   White planets wheeling by.

His trails are on the hillsides
   And down the dales and deeps;
He walks the high horizons
   Where vesper silence sleeps.

He haunts the lowly highways
   Where human hopes have trod
The Via Dolorosa
   Up to the heart of God.

He looms, a lonely figure,
   Along the fringe of night,
As lonely as a cedar
   Against the lonely light.

Judean hills are holy,
   Judean fields are fair,
For one can find the footprints
   Of Jesus everywhere.
                WILLIAM L. STIDGER


## Symbols

I never see upon a hill
   Cedar, or pine, or olive tree,
But that I think of One who died
   On Calvary.

I never hear the hammer's ring
　　Driving the nail deep in the wood,
But that I see pale hands whose palms
　　Are red with blood.

I never feel the dark come down
　　But that I hear a piercing cry
That tears my heart. "*Eli ... Lama ...
　　Sabachthani!*"
　　　　　JOHN RICHARD MORELAND

*vivid*

## Reincarnation

From hills that echo strangely clear
The voice of Jesus hovers near,
Yearning to live again in hands
Obedient to love's commands,
Assured our every breath and stride
Will mold the dream for which he died.
　　　　　LLOYD FRANK MERRELL

## Praesto

Expecting Him, my door was open wide:
Then I looked around
If any lack of service might be found,
And saw Him at my side:
How entered, by what secret stair,
I know not, knowing only He was there.
　　　　　THOMAS EDWARD BROWN

### Immortal Words

Above the Lake of Galilee
Soft winds are blowing still,
With lyric words of love set free
Above the Lake of Galilee.
They blow across the timeless sea,
Immortal words that thrill.
Above the Lake of Galilee
Soft winds are blowing still.

ALINE BADGER CARTER

### In Palestine

Have the rocks on the hillside voices—
  And the clods under trampling feet?
Do the cobblestones utter a message,
  And the pebbles tell secrets sweet?

Yes, the hills and the vales have voices,
  The rocks by the wayside speak:
They tell of the march of the ages,
  And of Him whom the nations seek.

GEORGE W. CARLIN

## Pentecost

In simple wise the revelation came—
Upon a day of grief, and blind despair
Wherein the thorn-wreathed brow and wounded hands
Flashed into sudden meaning; then and there
The distant Christ drew close—a Friend new found!
"Lo—and thou, also!" sang the shining air!

LAURA SIMMONS

## To the Tomb

This morning I went to the tomb
To find the Christ.
In the dull light of the room
I sought the Sacrificed.
In old rituals, in quiet forms,
By old altars I bent
Like one who warms
His hands by dead fires. A sacrament
Of beauty I found—the tomb.

This morning I went to the tomb and bowed
Before old traditions, and dead.
Outside in the midst of the crowd
One man spoke with lifted head:
"Why seek the living among the dead?

He walks the road to Galilee
Breathing the perfume of early flowers.
He hears the song of the birds. He sings
In tune with men. The dark hours
He misses the bird that wings
Its daytime course. But in the night—
His presence is the light."

RAYMOND KRESENSKY


## Come Unto Me

We labor and are heavy-laden. Where
Shall we find rest unto our souls? We bleed
On thorn and flint, and rove in pilgrim weed
From shrine to shrine, but comfort is not there.
What went we out into thy desert bare,
O Human Life, to see? Thy greenest reed
Is Love, unmighty for our utmost need,
And shaken with the wind of our despair.
A voice from Heaven like dew on Hermon falleth,
That voice whose passion paled the olive leaf
In thy dusky aisles, Gethsemane, thou blest
Of gardens. 'Tis the Man of Sorrows calleth,
The Man of Sorrows and acquaint with grief:
"Come unto Me, and I will give you rest."

KATHARINE LEE BATES

### The Untried Door

Behold, we stand at many doors and knock;
    From house to house we pass in the cold night!
But hear not any creaking of the lock
    And through no crevice see the welcome light!

Silent those palaces for evermore!
    Only one house remains untried, where stands
The Friend, who waits our knocking on the door—
    Upon the latch his scarred and eager hands.
                          Edward Shillito


### He Is the Lonely Greatness

He is the lonely greatness of the world—
    (His eyes are dim),
His power it is holds up the cross
    That holds up him.

He takes the sorrow of the threefold hour—
    (His eyelids close)
Round him and round the wind—his Spirit—where
    It listeth blows.

And so the wounded greatness of the world
    In silence lies—
And death is shattered by the light from out
    Those darkened eyes.
                        Madeleine Caron Rock

### From "The May Queen"

He taught me all the mercy, for he show'd me all the sin.
Now, tho' my lamp was lighted late, there's One will let *converted*
    me in.

*at end of life*

ALFRED TENNYSON

### Faith

*I know He lives —*
*external evidences*
*unnecessary.*

I did not see the crown
He wore,
Nor touched the wounds
Of One who died,
Nor saw the rock that sealed
The door,
Nor comforted the ones
Who cried.

Yet, I believe Christ lives,
Although
I never found
The empty tomb;
Even today he lives,
I know. . . .
I saw a shadow
In my room.

DONALD EARL EDWARDS

## I See His Blood Upon the Rose

I see his blood upon the rose
    And in the stars the glory of his eyes,
His Body gleams amid eternal snows,
    His tears fall from the skies.

I see his face in every flower;
    The thunder and the singing of the birds
Are but his voice—and carven by his power
    Rocks are his written words.

All pathways by his feet are worn,
    His strong heart stirs the ever-beating sea,
His crown of thorns is twined with every thorn,
    His cross is every tree.

                    JOSEPH MARY PLUNKETT

## From "Pauline"

O thou pale form, . . .

.    .    .    .    .    .    .    .    .    .

. . . oft have I stood by thee—
Have I been keeping lonely watch with thee
In the damp night by weeping Olivet,
Or leaning on thy bosom, . . .
Or dying with thee on the lonely cross,
Or witnessing thine outburst from the tomb.

                    ROBERT BROWNING

### Christ Can Give Thee Heart                X

But Christ can give thee heart who loveth thee:  *yes he can*
Can set thee in the eternal ecstasy  *joy — "unspeakable"*
Of his great jubilee:
Can give thee dancing heart and shining face,
And lips filled full of grace,
(And pleasures of the rivers and the sea.
Who knocketh at his door
He welcomes evermore:
Kneel down before
That ever-open door  *— Heb 4:16*
(The time is short) and smite
Thy breast, and pray with all thy might.

CHRISTINA G. ROSSETTI

*abundant*


### Faith

Religion is of faith indeed,
    In God and life and Jesus Christ—
I wrote my name unto this creed,  *I subscribed*
    And still my need went unsufficed.

But when I turned aside from prayer
    To make another's need my own,  *Heb 13:1-2*
Lo! Christ and God were standing there,  *become reality*
    And Faith stood up in flesh and bone.  *Matt. 25*

HUGH O. ISBELL

*in Jesus*

*Thy neighbor —*

*you don't believe in a vacuum — but in relationship to others*

## Beneath Such Rains

The day I rode through Devonshire
  The lonely downs were dark with rain,
And all the Dorset fields a blur
  Of dripping hedge and dreary lane.

The sea was very near. The air
  Was damp and from a shifting sky.
Only one thing was lovely there
  And good to travelers going by.

The purple patches of the heather
  Held me like song, and I would go
Through all the dull and weary weather
  Thinking Who might have seen them so,

Thinking Who might have come this way
  With laughing breath and splashing hurry
Beneath such rains, on such a day
  To reach his hut at Glastonbury.
                              JAMES E. WARREN, JR.

[*Note: According to an old legend, Jesus, as a boy, visited
England with Joseph of Arimathea, who was a merchant.
Christ built a hut at Glastonbury, and, after the crucifixion, it was to this spot that Joseph brought what was to be
called the Holy Grail.*]

*as from the death & life -- grind meaning purpose.*

## To Him Who Walks the Water          XX *Tremendous,*

We sink within this earth's dark waters: we
Sink, human, in our deeper Galilee;                    *existentialism*
Alone, we drown within that bitter wave
Where very life itself becomes our grave.
Then Christ, who walks the waters as the land,
Touches our faltering hand with his firm hand—
And lo! we walk upon the drifting sea — *of sea.*
Of time, made steadfast with eternity. — *things unshakeable*
To Thee, O Christ, Thy drowning creatures cry:          *Heb*
"O save us from the lives by which we die!"

E. MERRILL ROOT


## Even as the Bird          X *In Him is our trust*

My soul's a new-fledged bird: it tries to fly—
Frightened—across the unseen fact of sky;
Forgetting, or not knowing, that the air—
The Christ by which it flies—is everywhere.

E. MERRILL ROOT


## "Launch Out Into the Deep"

All night they toiled, those men of Galilee,
Casting their heavy nets into the sea
And, taking nothing, when dawn stained the sky,
They made for shore, prepared their nets to dry.

"Launch out into the deep." A Voice they knew
Dispelled their gloom, their courage winged anew.

"Launch out." His words in this grim day become
A challenge to vast depths the soul may plumb,
Where love and service, comfort, joy and peace
Shall overflow the cup and still increase.

"Launch out. Let down the nets." That Voice again
Brings hope to lift the troubled hearts of men.

IDA NORTON MUNSON

## Vision

We by no shining Galilean lake
Have toiled, but long and little fruitfully
In waves of a more old and bitter sea
Our nets are cast; large winds, that sleep and wake,
Around the feet of dawn and sunset, make
Our spiritual inhuman company,
And formless shadows of water rise and flee,
All night, around us till the morning break.

Thus our lives wear—shall it be ever thus?
Some idle day, when least we look for grace,
Shall we see stand upon the shore indeed
The visible Master, and the Lord of us,
And leave our nets, nor question of his creed,
Following the Christ within a young man's face?

EDWARD DOWDEN

## Bartimeus

God, grant to us Thy blessed Gift again,
To walk with us, as once in Galilee—
Talking of pebbles, and of birds o'erhead;
Of little children, and our daily bread—
To us, Thy lowly fisher-folk! Make plain
The shining wonder of himself again
That we may touch the seamless garment's hem,
And be made whole of selfishness and sin;
Behold, the hearts made humble and contrite—
Lord, that we may at last receive our sight!

LAURA SIMMONS

## Fishers

Tangled in nets
Of our wild philosophy,
Caught in the backlash
Of ideas ill-cast,
Heaving the lead
Into unplumbed infinity,
Baffled, we stand
Beside the shore at last.
Snagged barbs, snarled lines,
Torn sails! What fishers we!
Teach us Thy skill,
O Man of Galilee.

ALBERT REGINALD GOLD

*Apart from thee we can do nothing*

## Life

O Love triumphant over guilt and sin,
My Soul is soiled, but Thou shalt enter in;
My feet must stumble if I walk alone,
Lonely my heart, till beating by Thine own,
My will is weakness till it rest in Thine,
Cut off, I wither, thirsting for the Vine,    *Jn 15*
My deeds are dry leaves on a sapless tree,
My life is lifeless till it live in Thee!

FREDERICK LAWRENCE KNOWLES

## Wayside Shrine

*has meaning to some people*

A wooden Christ within a wayside shrine
Looks down a mountain road, a deep ravine.
The air that once was sweet with spruce and pine
Is smoke and powder and the town between
The mountain slopes is bursting into flame.
O Christ upon a wayside cross, look down!
This valley will not ever be the same.
New buildings will arise upon this town.
Through war-wracked days stand firm, for there will be
Eyes that are raised to you, their tears unshed—
Too intimate with horror—eyes that see
A Christ of pity and are comforted.
Endure these days that those who come may find
Courage to build again and peace of mind!

GERTRUDE RYDER BENNETT

## In No Strange Land

O world invisible, we view thee,
O world intangible, we touch thee,
O world unknowable, we know thee,
Inapprehensible, we clutch thee!

Does the fish soar to find the ocean,
The eagle plunge to find the air—
That we ask of the stars in motion
If they have rumor of thee there?

Not where the wheeling systems darken,
And our benumbed conceiving soars!—
The drift of pinions, would we hearken,
Beats at our own clay-shuttered doors.

The angels keep their ancient places;—
Turn but a stone, and start a wing!
'Tis ye, 'tis your estrangèd faces,
That miss the many-splendored thing.

But (when so sad thou canst not sadder)
Cry;—and upon thy so sore loss
Shall shine the traffic of Jacob's ladder
Pitched betwixt Heaven and Charing Cross.

Yea, in the night, my Soul, my daughter,
Cry,—clinging Heaven by the hems;
And lo, Christ walking on the water
Not of Gennesareth, but Thames!

FRANCIS THOMPSON

## Most Honored Guest

Since he will call some night to sup
I must re-stock
My larder; fill again the cup;
Have all in readiness against the time
When he shall knock.

I shall, with pious hands, prepare
The oaten flour,
And serve a loaf to grace the fare
For him, who comes to break the bread
In that glad hour.

WALTER SHEA

## In the Way of Peace

Jesus, whose love rekindles dying fires
   Flickering to ashes in our aching hearts,
Be Thou the goal of all our best desires,
   The dawn from which our longing ne'er departs.

When night's grim loneliness throbs like a wound
   And day's bright sunshine stabs us like a sword,
Us, with Thy peace, like traveler's cloak, around,
   Enfold as we go forward, O our Lord.

Through the sharp thorns that lie along our way
   Make Thou a path for tired and bleeding feet,
And bring us to the wonder of that day
   When Love and Memory in Thee shall meet.

LAUCHLAN MACLEAN WATT

### From "Progress"

The Master stood upon the Mount, and taught.
He saw a fire in his disciples' eyes;
"The old law," they cried, "is wholly come to nought,
   Behold the new world rise!"

"Was it," the Lord then said, "with scorn ye saw
The old law observed by Scribes and Pharisees?
I say unto you, see *ye* keep that law
   More faithfully than these!

"Too hasty heads for ordering worlds, alas!
Think not that I to annul the law have will'd;
No jot, no tittle from the law shall pass,
   Till all shall be fulfill'd."

So Christ said eighteen hundred years ago.
And what then shall be said to those today
Who cry aloud to lay the old world low
   To clear the new world's way?

 .   .   .   .   .   .   .   .   .   .

"Say ye: 'The spirit of man has found new roads,
And we must leave the old faiths, and walk therein'?—
Leave then the Cross as ye have left carved gods,
   But guard the fire within!

"Bright else and fast the stream of life may roll,
And no man may the other's hurt behold;
Yet each will have one anguish—his own soul
   Which perishes of cold."

MATTHEW ARNOLD

## A River of Grace

Make of my heart an upper room, I pray,
  Swept clean of pride, let self be but a door
Through which young lives may come to Thee this day
  To know Thee as they have not known before.

Speak through my voice that they may hear Thine own.
  Shine through my life in beauty and in truth
That they may see the Comrade Christ alone
  And in the glad impulsiveness of youth

Rise up as did those fisher lads of Thine
  Who left their boats and nets to follow Thee,
So may they walk beside Thee, these of mine
  Whom out of all the world "Thou gavest me."

                              MOLLY ANDERSON HALEY


## The True Gift

I gave a beggar from my scanty store
Of hard-earned gold. He spent the shining ore
And came again, and yet again, still cold
  And hungry, as before.

I gave the Christ, and through that Christ of mine
He found himself, a man, supreme, divine,
Fed, clothed, and crowned with blessings manifold,
  And now he begs no more.

                                 ANONYMOUS

## Communion Hymn

His gospel sounds in every wind that sings,
  His footprints linger where he never trod,
Because he took life's elemental things
  And held them up to God.

So we recall him: in a cattle stable,
  In fisher's boats, beside a leper's bed;
And how he sat one fateful night at table
  And blessed our daily bread.

WILLIAM GAY

## The Carpenter of Galilee

The Carpenter of Galilee
  Comes down the street again,
In every land, in every age,
  He still is building men.

On Christmas Eve we hear him knock;
  He goes from door to door:
"Are any workmen out of work?
  The Carpenter needs more."

HILDA W. SMITH

## The Man of Sorrows

Christ claims our help in many a strange disguise;
Now, fever-ridden, on a bed he lies;
Homeless he wanders now beneath the stars;
Now counts the number of his prison bars;
Now bends beside us, crowned with hoary hairs.
No need have we to climb the heavenly stairs,
And press our kisses on his feet and hands;
In every man that suffers, he, the Man of
    Sorrows, stands!

ANONYMOUS

## Per Contra

They say Thou art a Myth—
    That every prayer is vain:
Yet still I seek Thee with
    My pleas, again, again.

"There is no Christ—nay, none!"
    The lips of men have said:
But see, Thou fabled One,
    I kiss the Hands that bled!

MAHLON LEONARD FISHER

### Dreams and Deeds

Dear Master, in Whose life I see
All that I long and fail to be;
Let Thy clear light forever shine
To shame and guide this life of mine.

Though what I dream and what I do
In my poor days are always two,
Help me, oppressed by things undone,
O Thou, Whose dreams and deeds were one.

JOHN HUNTER

### Vinco

*(A reply to the "Invictus" of W. E. Henley)*

Out of the depths, from cleft to cleft
  Toiling upward, my couch a stone,
I thank Thee, God, I am not left
  To face my soul's grim foes alone.

For damning fault and blacker guilt
  That flaunt the pathless wastes I strayed,
I had no plea save that which built
  Its hope on mercy Love has made.

I yearn to part the curtained years,
  To reach my loved one in that Land,
And through the turmoil of my tears
  To see life whole, and understand.

In other might I make my boast
And, dauntless, press the distant goal:
Great Victor of the conquering host,
Thou art the Captain of my soul.

ELLIOT FIELD

*[handwritten: Xst given all of life; the world new meaning, life abundant]*

## The Rhythm of His Life

*[handwritten marginal note: He is the key to beauty in nature]*

Until I caught the rhythm of his life,
I had not heard the music of the spheres,
The simple cadences of ancient psalms,
The lyric beauty of a thousand years.

I had not seen the loveliness of dawn
Across the lifted hills, the gold and gray
Of winter sunsets, or the moonlight's hush
Upon a sleeping world, or flash of spray

Against eternal rocks! And now, behold!
The Voiceless Future is a singing flame!
White Presences attend me everywhere, *[handwritten: angels]*
Their canticles an echo of his name!

MARY HALLET

## The Potion

*[handwritten marginal note: give me some joy!]*

Life's burnished grail I take from him—
A chalice I must drain from brim
Clear down to acid, dreggy stem;

Shall I complain if it be filled
With gall, or brine from tears distilled?
Nay, Lord, I'll drink what Thou hast willed.

But, God, of Thy love give me this sign:
Sometimes let laughter, fragrant, fine,
Make of the draught a bubbling wine.
WINNIE LYNCH ROCKETT

## Prayer

*We cannot but turn back to god — after wandering*

Bear with me, Master, when I turn from Thee.
Pity me in my loss.
Forgive me, knowing I shall come again
As certainly as day that follows night.
Steel magnetized will ever seek the pole,
So I, of my free will which is not free,
But in its very nature bent to Thine,
Will come to rest in Thee.
I, the swinging needle in the compass of the world;
Thou, the perpetual North.
EDITH LOVEJOY PIERCE

*The "imago Dei" not freedom —*

## "In Him Ye Are Made Full"

*Cross — now a symbol of life — not death. So is the grain of us.*

O empty cross, portentous against the sky,
Who, anguished, hung upon thine arms to die?
Who thus transformed thee from a thing of dread
To be a symbol of God's love instead?

O empty tomb, within a garden still,
Who lay within thine undefeated will? *death*
Who overcame thee as a seed the clay,
To rise victorious at the dawn of day?

O empty heart, despoiled by death and sin,
He comes with life and love to enter in;
For by his cross and tomb he conquered strife,
And fills you now with everlasting life.

WILLIAM H. HUDNUT, SR.

## A Prayer for the Presence of Christ

*at Communion*

Reveal Thy Presence now, O Lord,
  As in the Upper Room of old;
Break Thou our bread, grace Thou our board,
  And keep our hearts from growing cold.

THOMAS TIPLADY

## I Would Go Back

*To be alone with Jesus
& be taught by Him*

XX

I would go back and sit beside his feet, *Amen!*
  Far from the swaying arguments of men,
So, listening to the cadence sweet
  Of that dear Voice, would know the truth as then.

How simple, just to lean in that quiet place,
  Remote from controversy and vexed strife,
And hear, rapt, gazing upward on his face,
  Fall from his lips the jeweled words of life.

Not where men's errors, subtly wove, disclose
  A glittering Serpent that uprears and stings
Till hearts are broke—but here the spirit grows
  'Mid mountain peace, and brooding sense of wings.

What is the Faith that I shall call for mine,
  Creed of my fathers, reverenced in my heart?
Nay, far more high, more sacred, more divine—
  That boundless Love Christ teacheth far apart.

                                    MARY M. CURCHOD

## Failure

I strove, O Lord, to grasp a star for Thee,
And, falling, clutched the dust. "That bit of earth
Upon your palm is of a starry worth,"
I heard Thee say: "Give that instead to me!"

I thought in knightly quest or holy wars
To win Thee treasure. Bowed on a broken sword
I cried, "My hands are empty." Thou, O Lord,
Didst answer, "Nay, you bring a gift of scars."

Lord, I have sought Thy face in vain, and now
I weary. Ah, where art Thou? Hark! I hear
Thy voice: "You sought me, therefore I will wear
Your darkness as a light about my brow."

                                    MARY SINTON LEITCH

*Comfort us!*

## Christ and the Mourners

Down on the shadowed stream of time and tears
Voice of new grief and grief of ancient years—
Sad as when first from loving lips 'twas sighed—
"Hadst Thou been here, my brother had not died."

Comfort us, Lord, who heard'st poor Martha's plaint,
Heal the sore heart, uplift the spirit faint—
O Thou, the Peace that cometh after strife!
O Thou, the Resurrection and the Life!

KATHERINE E. CONWAY

*Prays for light & understanding!*

## Thou Light of Ages

Thou Light of Ages, Source of living truth,
　Shine into every groping, seeking mind;
Let plodding age and pioneering youth
　Each day some clearer, brighter pathway find.

Thou Light of Ages, shining forth in Christ,
　Whose brightness darkest ages could not dim,
Grant us the spirit which for him sufficed—
Rekindle here the torch of love for him.

ROLLAND W. SCHLOERB

## Faith

*mystery*

And must I say that God is Christ
  Or Jesus God in human guise,
When I can say he has sufficed *He bro't God to me.*
  To bring the light to shadowed eyes?

I do not care to speculate
  On things mysterious to the mind;
But O the rapture, early, late
  Of light to eyes that once were blind.

EDWIN McNEILL POTEAT

## Victory *I thn.*

To him that overcometh,
  John the Beloved said,
Is given the hidden manna *new life; on the*
  To be his daily bread. *Lord's prayer.*

I drank Thy burning honey,
  Lord Jesus, long ago;
And still my heart goes hungry
  For all I do not know.

But, O my Lord, I thank Thee,
  I kiss Thy wounded feet;
To him that overcometh
  The common day is sweet!

MARGUERITE WILKINSON

*wonderful.*

### From "Abide in Me" *we need Him for everyhour.*

The soul alone, like a neglected harp,
  Grows out of tune, and needs that Hand divine;
Dwell Thou within it! tune and touch the chord,
  Till every note and string shall answer Thine!

Abide in me,—There have been moments pure
  When I have seen Thy face and felt Thy power;
Then evil lost its grasp, and passion, hushed,
  Owned the divine enchantment of the hour. *a prayer.*

HARRIET BEECHER STOWE


### Faith

It is the road, the chart,
The wafer and the wine;
Who lives by faith
Shall find life good
And clutch the things divine.

*Heb //*

Christ and his word shall be
Their sustenance till breath
Slips from the clay—
Who lives by faith
Shall never taste of death.

JOHN RICHARD MORELAND

## New Gethsemane

Now once again the Christ keeps watch beside
The sick-bed of the world; once more he kneels
Within the Garden; once again he feels *Suffering God*
Vicariously man's sinning as a tide *- Weatherhead*
Of mighty waters, deep and cold and wide!
Do you recall, as gathering night conceals
His presence, as the lengthening shadow steals
Across his heart, how once before he cried:
"Can ye not watch with me one hour?" The sword
Is close upon us, yet we fall asleep—
A recreant discipleship impressed *we-sleepers.*
Too lightly! Wake us from our slumbering, Lord,
Before the hour has come and we too reap
The judgment—"Sleep on now and take your rest."

HAZEL M. KERR

## Give Our Conscience Light *good*

Shine forth into the night, O Flame
Of Love. The world is lost
In chaos. Heap the war-crime blame
On us till Pentecost
Will come again with tongues of fire
To burn upon our heads.

Let our last breath of greed expire
Until new vision spreads
Like waking dawn when earth began.
Oh give us God-filled sight!
Shine forth through darkness, Son of Man,
And give our conscience light.

ALINE BADGER CARTER


## Angel Voices

Listen! Do you hear the winging
    Chorus of an angel choir?
All the hosts of heaven are singing,
And earth's rafters fill with ringing
    Like a huge celestial lyre.

See, the monotones of sorrow
    Melt in music at his birth,
Christ, who teaches men to borrow
From the fullness of tomorrow
    Peace, good will for all the earth.

Angel voices, sent to woo us,
    Carol in the skies again.
Love is Victor; Love that drew us,
Love that ever whispers to us:
    "Peace on earth, good will to men."

MARY B. STEVENSON

### Christmas Bells

I heard the bells on Christmas day
Their old familiar carols play,
   And wild and sweet
   The word repeat,
Of "Peace on earth, good will to men!"

And thought how, as the day had come,
The belfries of all Christendom
   Had rolled along
   The unbroken song,
Of "Peace on earth, good will to men!"

Till ringing, singing on its way,
The world revolved from night to day,—
   A voice, a chime,
   A chant sublime,
Of "Peace on earth, good will to men!"

.    .    .    .    .    .    .    .

Then pealed the bells more loud and deep;
"God is not dead; nor doth he sleep!
   The wrong shall fail,
   The right prevail,
With peace on earth, good will to men!"
        HENRY WADSWORTH LONGFELLOW

## Who Are the Wise Men?

Who were the Wise Men in the long ago?
Not Herod, fearful lest he lose his throne;
Not Pharisees too proud to claim their own;
Not priests and scribes whose province was to know;
Not money-changers running to and fro;
But three who traveled, weary and alone,
With dauntless faith, because before them shone
The Star that led them to a manger low.

Who are the Wise Men now, when all is told?
Not men of science; not the great and strong;
Not those who wear a kingly diadem;
Not those whose eager hands pile high the gold;
But those amid the tumult and the throng
Who follow still the Star of Bethlehem.

B. Y. WILLIAMS

## Query

The world is the Inn at Bethlehem
    And still for the Little One no room.
Peace is a flower with a broken stem.
   (When will his world-wide unity bloom?

LUCIA TRENT

## To the Christ

Thou hast on earth a Trinity—
Thyself, my fellow man, and me:
When one with him, then one with Thee:
Nor, save together, Thine are we.

JOHN BANISTER TABB

## Live Christ

Live Christ!—and though the way may be
In this world's sight adversity,
He who doth heed thy every need
Shall give thy soul prosperity.

Live Christ!—and though the road may be
The narrow street of poverty,
He had not where to lay his head,
Yet lived in largest liberty.

Live Christ!—and though the road may be
The straight way of humility,
He who first trod that way of God
Will clothe thee with his dignity.

Live Christ!—and though thy life may be
In much a valedictory,
The heavy cross brings seeming loss,
But wins the crown of victory.

Live Christ!—and all thy life shall be
    A High Way of Delivery—
A Royal Road of goodly deeds,
    Gold-paved with sweetest charity.

Live Christ!—and all thy life shall be
    A sweet uplifting ministry,
A sowing of the fair white seeds
    That fruit through all eternity.

JOHN OXENHAM

## The Universal Language

The wise men ask, "What language did Christ speak?"
    They cavil, argue, search, and little prove.
O Sages, leave your Syriac and your Greek!
    Christ spoke the universal language—Love.

ELLA WHEELER WILCOX

## The Trimmed Lamp

I dare not slight the stranger at my door—
    Threadbare of garb and sorrowful of lot—
Lest it be Christ that stands; and goes his way
    Because I, all unworthy, knew him not.

I dare not miss one flash of kindling cheer
    From alien souls, in challenge glad and high.
Ah, what if God be moving very near
    And I, so blind, so deaf, had passed him by?

LAURA SIMMONS

## As Ye Do It Unto These *Mt 24*

In little faces pinched with cold and hunger
Look, lest ye miss him! In the wistful eyes,
And on the mouths unfed by mother kisses, *orphans*
Marred, bruised and stained his precious image lies!
And when ye find him in the midnight wild,
Even in the likeness of an outcast child,
O wise men, own your King!
Before his cradle bring
Your gold to raise and bless,
Your myrrh of tenderness,
For, "As ye do it unto these," said he,
"Ye do it unto me."

ANONYMOUS

## Dedication for a Home

O Thou whose gracious presence blest
    The home at Bethany,
This shelter from the world's unrest,
This home made ready for its Guest,
    We dedicate to Thee.

We build an altar here, and pray
    That Thou wilt show Thy face.
Dear Lord, if Thou wilt come to stay,
This home we consecrate today
    Will be a holy place.

JOHN OXENHAM

## Hymn for a Household

Lord Christ, beneath Thy starry dome
We light this flickering lamp of home,
And where bewildering shadows throng
Uplift our prayer and evensong.
Dost Thou, with heaven in Thy ken,
Seek still a dwelling place with men,
Wandering the world in ceaseless quest?
O Man of Nazareth, be our guest!

Lord Christ, the bird his nest has found,
The fox is sheltered in his ground,
But dost Thou still this dark earth tread
And have no place to lay Thy head?
Shepherd of mortals, here behold
A little flock, a wayside fold
That wait Thy presence to be blest—
O Man of Nazareth, be our guest!

DANIEL HENDERSON

## Prayer Before Meat

Christ, by dark clouds of worldliness concealed,
Stand in the breaking of this bread revealed;
Feeling Thy tender presence let us guard
Each cruel thought, each bitter, unkind word.
Linked here by bonds of love, now let us feed
Upon Thy grace and find it meat indeed.

UNA W. HARSEN

## Christ in Woolworths

I did not think to find You there—
Crucifixes, large and small,
Sixpence and threepence, on a tray,
Among the artificial pearls,
Paste rings, tin watches, beads of glass.
It seemed so strange to find You there
Fingered by people coarse and crass,
Who had no reverence at all.
Yet—what is it that You would say?
"For these I hang upon My cross,
For these the agony and loss,
Though heedlessly they pass Me by."
Dear Lord, forgive such fools as I,
Who thought it strange to find You there,
When You are with us everywhere.

Teresa Hooley

## The Living Tithe

Ten met the Master in a field,
Called to him, agonized, were healed.
Nine hastened on their various ways.
One only, cleansed, returned to praise
Lettered in gratitude and grace,
Meeting his Master face to face.

Let me give thanks! O number me
Among that lesser company.

Mabel Munns Charles

*Good prayer for housewife.*

### Prayer Hymn

Lord of all pots and pans and things, since I've no time
    to be
A Saint by doing lovely things, or watching late with
    Thee,
Or dreaming in the dawnlight, or storming Heaven's
    gates,
Make me a saint by getting meals, and washing up the
    plates.

Although I must have Martha's hands, I have a Mary
    mind;
And when I black the boots and shoes, Thy sandals, Lord,
    I find.
I think of how they trod the earth, what time I scrub the
    floor;
Accept this meditation, Lord, I haven't time for more.

Warm all the kitchen with Thy love, and light it with
    Thy peace;
Forgive me all my worrying, and make all grumbling
    cease.
Thou who didst love to give men food, in room, or by
    the sea,
Accept this service that I do—I do it unto Thee.

                              M. K. H.

*Phil.*

## Jesus of Nazareth Passes By

*See Christ now glorified as Sovereign*
*King of kings; how / how*
*cf. Isa. 6*

Unshaken by the storms that rage
  O'er all the earth, in every time,
Moves one lone Man through every age,
  Serene, invincible, sublime.
Through all the centuries he goes,
  His timeless journey to complete,
Divinely calm, as one who knows
  The way is sure beneath his feet.

Wild storms of hate beat round his head,
  Earth rocks beneath the crash of war,
But still, with smooth, unhurried tread,
  He moves, untroubled as before.
Over the wrecks of fallen states,
  Through fair, proud nations yet to fall,
Passes the Master of their fates,
  The silent Sovereign of them all.

Unfaltering through the darkest night,
  Denied by man, though loving man,
His face gives back the morning light,
  His calm eyes see God's finished plan.
One little troubled day we bide,
  And then find rest in beds of clay;
But our brief day is glorified—
  We have seen Jesus pass this way. ) *Amen.*
                    GEORGE T. LIDDELL

*wonderful grace
at breaking of bread
& from.*

### Grace at Evening

Be with us, Lord, at eventide;
   Far has declined the day,
Our hearts have glowed
Along the road,
   Thou hast made glad our way.

Take Thou this loaf and bless it, Lord,
   And then with us partake;
Unveil our eyes
To recognize
   Thyself, for Thy dear sake. *Amen.*
             EDWIN McNEILL POTEAT

### The Housewife

*wonderful
for mothers*

Jesus, teach me how to be
Proud of my simplicity.

Sweep the floors, wash the clothes,
Gather for each vase a rose.

Iron and tend a tiny frock,
Keeping one eye on the clock.

Always having time kept free
For childish questions asked of me.

Grant me wisdom Mary had
When she taught her little Lad.
            CATHERINE CATE COBLENTZ

## The King Passes

The King has passed along the great highway
Where throngs of eager, curious crowds proclaim his
    praise;
I was so far away—indifferently I gazed,
When, lo! he spoke so clear
I heard as though quite near,
"Come unto Me all ye who labor, and I will give you
    rest." *I didn't know my need*

(And I, who labored not, longed to be blest.)
My heart awoke—my hands reached out and up.
I labor now, unceasingly,
To fill life's empty cup, *He called me into labor—only*
That he may stoop and give at last
The blessing promised, as he passed.

ANNE HUNTER TEMPLE

## Lent

Behold, we go up to Jerusalem again—
The long, hazardous climb, and then
The menacing city upon the hill;
It is time to go with Christ and his twelve men.

Let us all go up to Jerusalem, bend
The will to the tortuous way till the end—
Those of the curious gaze, the blind,
The sick, the lame by the road, betrayer and friend.

Let us go. The palms and the singing trees await
In Jerusalem, the greed and the hate;
The upper room and Gethsemane,
The judgment hall and death without the gate.

We shall run to the garden the third dawn
And, stooping, find that our Lord is gone
From the tomb; at the Voice, we shall turn and know
That the living Christ bids us rejoice and be on.

Every trail of the stars, of the earth and the sea,
The roads of the past, and those to be,
Christ walks on his way to Jerusalem;
And it is time to go up in his company.

Miriam LeFevre Crouse

## Still Thou Art Question

We place Thy sacred name upon our brows;
  Our cycles from Thy natal day we score:
Yet, spite of all our songs and all our vows,
  We thirst and ever thirst to know Thee more.

For Thou art Mystery and Question still;
  Even when we see Thee lifted as a sign
Drawing all men unto that hapless hill
  With the resistless power of Love Divine.

Still Thou art Question—while rings in our ears
  Thine outcry to a world discord-beset:
Have I been with thee all these many years,
  O World—dost thou not know Me even yet?

Anonymous

# The Revolutionist

# The Revolutionist

## The Blessed Agitator

Jesus, the Blessed Agitator,
Hung for hours on a cross
For a world of waving cornfields
And blossoming orchards.
Let us celebrate the Christ Militant.
Let us revere the Carpenter's Son,
Who drove the money-changers from the Temple.

Let us make the brotherhood he taught
Not a word in a minister's sermon
But rich bread on a child's plate
And coal in an old man's furnace.
Let us make the holy democracy of Jesus
Not a word in a dictionary
But a candle in each human soul,

*can you imagine!!*

*— live out ethics of gospel*

*U.S.A. way of life*

293

A light to cleanse the hate-ravaged world,
To make fertile the greed-harrowed earth.
Let us restore to the people,
Huddled and cowed under the lash of profiteer and ex-
    ploiter,
Their natural heritage.

Let us celebrate the Christ Militant,
Jesus, who died for a world of laughing children
And men and women with peace and love in their eyes.

LUCIA TRENT

### The Divine Rebel

The Carpenter was not afraid to die
For his convictions. Though he was reviled,
He would not stoop to safe conformity.
The synagogue, by wanton greed defiled,
He cleansed in spite of scribe and Pharisee.
To wrong and evil he refused to yield.

Because he preached of love and brotherhood,
He was by priest and Pilate crucified;
And only those who loved him understood
That when he died, revolt was sanctified. . . .
And we who brook the scheming powers-that-be
Live in his Rebel-Soul impregnably.

GEORGE SCHEFTEL

## The Christ Militant

We serve no weak and timid Christ,
  We would not heed a futile Lord;
The man we follow unto death
  Was not afraid of rod or sword.

He asked no pillow for his head,
  He sought no luxury of ease;
The tides that swept his daring soul
  Were dauntless as the mighty seas.

The little town of Nazareth
  Could never bound his spirit's aim;
He dreamed that every zone of earth
  Should know the wonder of his name.

A soldier of the truth was he;
  His anger flamed at vested wrong;
He challenged kings to fateful war,
  And sounded clear his battle song.

Against the cruel lords of pride
  He stood a warrior, strong and sure,
And whipped the greedy temple thieves
  Who sought to cheat his helpless poor.

He ruled the stubborn hearts of men,
  And yet disdained the tyrant's rod—
The mighty Captain of the Right,
  The Saviour of the World of God.

THOMAS CURTIS CLARK

*Social justice*      **A Parable**     XX *Tremendous.*

Said Christ our Lord, "I will go and see
How the men, my brethren, believe in Me."
He passed not again through the gate of birth,
But made himself known to the children of earth.

Then said the chief priests, and rulers, and kings,
"Behold, now, the Giver of all good things;
Go to, let us welcome with pomp and state
Him who alone is mighty and great."

*A story*

With carpets of gold the ground they spread
Wherever the Son of Man should tread,
And in palace chambers lofty and rare
They lodged him, and served him with kingly fare.

*Church*

Great organs surged through arches dim
Their jubilant floods in praise of him;
And in church, and palace, and judgment hall,
He saw his image high over all.

But still, wherever his steps they led,
The Lord in sorrow bent down his head,
And from under the heavy foundation stones
The son of Mary heard bitter groans.

And in church, and palace, and judgment hall
He marked great fissures that rent the wall,
And opened wider and yet more wide
As the living foundation heaved and sighed.

*These great edifices are built on exploitation of living people.*

"Have ye founded your thrones and altars, then,
On the bodies and souls of living men?
And think ye that building shall endure
Which shelters the noble and crushes the poor?

"With gates of silver and bars of gold
Ye have fenced my sheep from the Father's fold;
I have heard the dropping of their tears
In heaven these eighteen hundred years."

"O Lord and Master, not ours the guilt,
We built but as our fathers built;
Behold Thine images, how they stand,
Sovereign and sole, through all our land.

"Our task is hard—with sword and flame
To hold Thine earth forever the same,
And with sharp crooks of steel to keep
Still, as Thou leftest them, Thy sheep."

Then Christ sought out an artisan,
A low-browed, stunted, haggard man,
And a motherless girl, whose fingers thin
Pushed from her faintly want and sin.

Them set he in the midst of them,
And as they drew back their garment-hem,
For fear of defilement, "Lo, here," said he,
The images ye have made of Me!"

                              JAMES RUSSELL LOWELL

## A Virile Christ

Give us a virile Christ for these rough days!
You painters, sculptors, show the warrior bold;
And you who turn mere words to gleaming gold,
Too long your lips have sounded in the praise
Of patience and humility. Our ways
Have parted from the quietude of old;
We need a man of strength with us to hold
The very breach of Death without amaze.
Did he not scourge from temple courts the thieves?
And make the arch-fiend's self again to fall?
And blast the fig-tree that was only leaves?
And still the raging tumult of the seas?
Did he not bear the greatest pain of all,
Silent, upon the cross on Calvary?

REX BOUNDY

*These N.T.
incidents
show a Christ
many men
need—in order
to appreciate
Him.*

## The Unlikely Rebel

A most unlikely rebel, he,
This simple man from Galilee—
A carpenter who dared to dream!

A carpenter who dared to dream
And in the half-light saw the gleam
Of flashing swords within men's hearts—

Bright swords of truth within men's hearts
All readied to play noble parts
In hands upheld by faith and grace.

Strong hands, like his, with faith and grace
Can wield these swords in any place
Till Caesar roars and Caiaphas shakes.

Yes, Caesar roars and Caiaphas shakes—
For truth, of any rebel, makes
A foe implacable!

*Give us truth; we'll die for it*

FRANKLIN D. ELMER, JR.


## Upon This Rock

O Carpenter of Nazareth,
Of lowliest birth, of bitterest death,
A workman, and the workman's friend,
When will the worker's Calvary end?

*capital : labor.*

Thou who art named the Prince of Peace,
When will the reign of Caesars cease?
When will the warring legions pass,
And all the strife of caste and class?

They call Thee God, but make Thee fool
Who laud the soul and damn the tool;
Who make Thee sovereign of the skies
But build Thee here a House of Lies.

*work*   *God glorifies work*

When men are labor-born today,
Where labor walks Golgotha's way,
Where workmen share Thy workman's smock—
Where else Thy Church, who else Thy Rock?

*The working man - the true Church*

All other Rocks have proven sand;
All other Churches fouled Thy hand.
Thy fellow workers of the earth
Are come to give Thy Kingdom birth.

ROBERT WHITAKER

## Futile Sacrifice

The Lamb of God wears a scarlet robe,
   And thorns have pierced his eyes,
As he walks abroad in the dying world
   In sacrificial disguise.

For the Lamb of God has taken our sins—
   The sins of the world of men—
And he staggers blindly along blind streets
   Seeking the Sword again.

The Sword of his God, of our God, which strikes
   In a flashing stream of light,
And the Lamb of God would wield his Sword
   To banish our ignorant night.

But we turn away from his bloody form,
   And we hide our eyes from his shame—
We would grovel, yet, in our gross despair,
   Rather than speak his Name.

And the Lamb of God walks on, walks on,
   With his robe and his thorn-pierced eyes,
Seeking, seeking the Sword of Truth
   In the streets of mortal lies.

MURRAY SKINNER

*excellent — Christ powerless we render by our unbelief.*

## To a Revolutionist

XX

With deadly drive Your grim advance    *my sermon —*
Against tradition swept the world.
But we have found a way to conquer even You.
We talk like rebels, deprecate tradition,
Discuss with unchanged hearts a world of change,    *True*
And make of You, tradition-smashing Christ,
Another dead tradition!

HAROLD E. FEY

## Mary's Son

Jesus, the friend of lonely, beaten folk,
  Comrade, defender of each humble one,
Who put Your generous shoulders to the yoke)
  That we might live in nobler unison,

Why have we worshiped You with sword and flame,
  Placed You, a worker, on a regal throne
And let our brother's blood flow in Your name,
  Who loved all human creatures as Your own?

Let us remember You as Mary's son,
  A worker, seeking rights for men who toil,
Conscious that we are brothers every one    *lines on human*
  Upon the glowing earth's fraternal soil.    *brotherhood*

Let us remember You as one who died
For love of every comrade at his side.

LUCIA TRENT

## From "The Toiling of Felix"

Never in a costly palace did I rest on golden bed,
Never in a hermit's cavern have I eaten idle bread.

Born within a lowly stable where the cattle round Me
   stood,
Trained a carpenter of Nazareth, I have toiled and found
   it good.

They who tread the path of labor follow where My feet
   have trod; *Idleness is not Christian*
They who work without complaining do the Holy Will
   of God.

Where the many toil together, there am I among My own;
When the tired workman sleepeth, then am I with him
   alone.

I, the Peace that passeth knowledge, dwell amid the daily
   strife,
I, the Bread of Heaven, am broken in the sacrament of
   life.

HENRY VAN DYKE

## Crusaders

They have taken the tomb of our Comrade Christ—
   Infidel hordes that believe not in Man;
Stable and stall for him sufficed,
   But his tomb is built on a kingly plan.

They have hedged him round with pomp and parade,
  They have buried him deep under steel and stone—
But we come leading the great Crusade
  To give our Comrade back to his own.

*To give Christ back to the common people*

ELIZABETH WADDELL

## Jesus

The martyred Christ of the working class, the inspired
  evangel of the downtrodden masses, the world's supreme revolutionary leader,
Whose love for the poor and the children of the poor hallowed all the days of his consecrated life, lighted
  up and made forever holy the dark tragedy of his
  death, and gave to the ages his divine inspiration and
  his deathless name.

EUGENE V. DEBS

*He comes to purify our souls.*

## The Whip of Anger

Through the sea of money-changers he stormed.
The whip of his anger tore like wind
And upset wares piled wave high in his path.

Was this the gentle Christ of love and pity?
What crime has changed serenity to wrath?
His voice is thunder: *This is my Father's house!*

*yes — in that tone it was said*

Remembering this,
Remembering also words, Your soul a temple,
Do you dare the raging lightning in the eyes of God?

MARY ROSS

### Unemployed

"It's hard to be without a wage," I said,
   "It's worse to not be wanted, your work unpriced."
"I know too well," the man in the line ahead
   Spoke up. "And who are you?" "They call me Christ."

RALPH CHEYNEY

*The same helpfulness*
*at wisdom mens action that*
*2 at times feel.*

### Lore

X good.

Humanity struggles on and is blind—
Of the making of books there is no end:
Wisdom and Folly, striving, tend
To heap up the shelves, each with his kind.
Christ wrote a few words in the sand.

EDNA ETHEL DAVIS

### Young Warrior

Young Warrior, O young Warrior,
   Who kept Thy watch to death,
A whole world died in wonder
   With Thy last breath.

Eternal Youth, supply us
   With faith to see ahead
Beyond the final question
   Posed by the serried dead.

Then, in armor brighter
   Than a blinding star
Go forever forward
   Where no battles are.
                GEORGE EDWARD HOFFMAN


## Christ on Madison Street

I looked for Christ on Madison Street
Where men went by with stumbling feet,
Where heads were bowed in the darkness there
Of gray clouds hanging low in the air.

I looked for him, a vision of white—
But gay burlesques with their crimson light
Have led my steps to a darker place
Where smoke of passion hid Christ's face.

I looked for Christ in the hidden skies,
A flaming vision to blind my eyes—
While Christ walked by with stumbling feet
Along with the men of Madison Street.
                RAYMOND KRESENSKY


## His Throne Is With the Outcast

I followed where they led,
   And in a hovel rude,
With naught to fence the weather from his head,
   The King I sought for meekly stood;

A naked hungry child
  Clung round his gracious knee,
And a poor hunted slave looked up and smiled
  To bless the smile that set him free;
New miracles I saw his presence do,
  No more I knew the hovel bare and poor,
The gathered chips into a woodpile grew
  The broken morsel swelled to goodly store.
I knelt and wept: my Christ no more I seek.
His throne is with the outcast and the weak.

James Russell Lowell

"lift up thy countenance upon us"

## From "The Vision of Sir Launfal"

And the voice that was calmer than silence said,
"Lo it is I, be not afraid!
In many climes, without avail,
Thou hast spent thy life for the Holy Grail;
Behold, it is here—this cup which thou
Didst fill at the streamlet for me but now;
This crust is my body broken for thee,
This water His blood that died on the tree;
The Holy Supper is kept, indeed,
In whatso we share with another's need,—
Not that which we give, but what we share,—
For the gift without the giver is bare;
Who gives himself with his alms feeds three,
Himself, his hungering neighbor, and me."

James Russell Lowell

## Voice in a Cathedral

Is this the tribute you have brought to Me—
Who found My joy, sojourning on the earth,
In peasant fishermen? Who found more worth
In outcasts than a heart-proud Pharisee?
These massive walls, this gold-engraven door,
This stately aisle, are for a king's parade.
These jewel-studded altars—were they made
For Me, who loved the helpless and the poor?

Ye hypocrites, I loathe these blood-stained stones.
What is it that I hear? the cries of men
Enslaved by greed; a flooding tide of pain—
Of broken women—little children's groans!

Blaspheme no longer. Set My brethren free,
Then bring your Hallelujahs unto Me.

THOMAS CURTIS CLARK

## Master Surgeon

Men at the Council Tables,
The map of the world lies before you
Like a broken body.
You are the surgeons in consultation,
Stroking your beards,
Tapping your fingers.
Sharp words are shot from your lips,
Angry gestures flung from your hands.

The broken body tosses while you quarrel,
The broken body moans while you wrangle.

There is only One Surgeon who can heal.
His eyes are wide with compassion.
His mouth is soft with sympathy.
His hands . . . Look! Are they not spiked with nails?
He stands at your sides ready with his healing.
Seek him out and listen, men at the Council Tables,
For only his wisdom can heal
The broken, moaning body of the world.

LUCIA TRENT


## O Prophets and Redeemers!

O prophets and redeemers! you who bled
To clear man's pathway lest he trip and fall!
Confucius, Buddha, Moses, Christ, and all
Those luminous ones who loved our race, and led!
What voice have you against the rage and dread
Shaking our planet like a thunder call?
What word for us whom bombs and bones appall
On fields where only vultures' beaks are fed?

The hills are silent, and the stars are mute.
Yet even remembrance of those haloed souls
Uplifts the eyes, and spurs the flagging heart,
And makes us glimpse, beyond war's skull-marked fruit,
The silvery cloud-fringe of more lustrous goals,
The light that, kindled, cannot quite depart.

STANTON A. COBLENTZ

*[handwritten: Good. We excuse men; but let a woman fall — she's done for.]*

## What Our Lord Wrote in the Dust

We have saved the soul of the man who killed,
  We have turned to shrive the thief;
We restored the pride of the man who lied
  And we gave him our belief;
But for her who fell we have fashioned hell
  With a faith all stern and just—
It was so of old; and no man hath told
  What our Lord wrote in the dust.

We have sighed betimes for our brothers' crimes
  And have bade them be of cheer,
For the flesh is weak, and the soul grown meek
  May yet read its title clear.
But we draw away from the one astray
  As the truly righteous must,
She is cursed indeed—and we did not read
  What our Lord wrote in the dust.

For the men who thieved, and who killed and lied—
  Who have slain the woman's soul—
We have worked and prayed, and have seen them made
  All clean and pure and whole,
But we drive her out with a righteous shout
  In our Pharisaic trust,
So the man goes free—but we do not see
  What our Lord wrote in the dust.

ANONYMOUS

*very good*

## The Soul of Jesus Is Restless

The soul of Jesus is restless today;
Christ is tramping through the spirit-world,
Compassion in his heart for fainting millions;
He trudges through China, through Poland,
Through Russia, Austria, Germania, Armenia;
Patiently he pleads with the Church,
Tenderly he woos her.
The wounds of his body are bleeding afresh for the sor-
    rows of his shepherdless people.
We besiege him with selfish petitions,
We weary him with our petty ambitions,
From the needy we bury him in piles of carven stone, *Church*
We obscure him in the smoke of stuffy incense,
We drown his voice with the snarls and shrieks of our
    disgruntled bickerings,
We build temples to him with hands that are bloody,
We deny him in the needs and sorrows of the exploited
    "least of his brethren."
The soul of Jesus is restless today,
But eternally undismayed.

CYPRUS R. MITCHELL

### Not Made With Hands

Carpenter, what are you building now?
　　Have your still hands lost their art?
I am building a house not made with hands　X
　　Eternal in the heart.

Carpenter, what are you seeing now,
　　With your hammers lying still?
I see the temples of freedom rise,
　　Sheer from the rock of will.　）

Carpenter, what are you saying now?
　　Is it drowned in the planet's spin?
No sound can drown what the Chosen hear;
　　I am calling my Builders in.

I am calling the meek to inherit the earth,
　　I am trampling the serpent's spawn,
I am hewing the beams for the Ark of Peace
　　That will sail in the Golden Dawn.

LILITH LORRAINE

## Jesus

Jesus, whose lot with us was cast,
Who saw it out, from first to last;
Patient and fearless, tender, true,
Carpenter, vagabond, felon, Jew;
Whose humorous eye took in each phase
Of full, rich life this world displays,
Yet evermore kept fast in view
The far-off goal it leads us to;
Who, as your hour neared, did not fail—
The world's fate trembling in the scale—
With your half-hearted band to dine,
And chat across the bread and wine;
Then went out firm to face the end,
Alone, without a single friend;
Who felt, as your last words confessed,
Wrung from a proud, unflinching breast
By hours of dull, ignoble pain,
Your whole life's fight was fought in vain—
Would I could win and keep and feel
That heart of love, that spirit of steel!

ANONYMOUS

# The Lost Christ

# The Lost Christ

## He—They—We

They hailed him King as he passed by,
  They strewed their garments in the road,
But they were set on earthly things,
  And he on God.

They sang his praise for that he did,
  But gave his message little thought;
They could not see that their soul's good
  Was all he sought.

They could not understand why he,
  With powers so vast at his command,
Should hestitate to claim their rights
  And free the land.

315

*Mt 13*
*cares of world*

*good*

Their own concern and this world's hopes
  Shut out the wonder of his News;
And we, with larger knowledge, still
  His Way refuse.

He walks among us still, unseen,
  And still points out the only way,
But we still follow other gods
  And him betray.

JOHN OXENHAM

## Wanderers

Our feet have wandered from Thy path,
  Thou lowly Christ of Galilee,
Sweet prophet of the helping hand,
  Meek Lord of love and sympathy.

Thy faith was but to walk with God
  With humble heart and open mind,
But we have builded shrines of stone
  In which to worship—spirit-blind!

We lift our heads in loveless prayers,
  We glory in our well-wrought creed,
Though righteousness alone avails,
  Though mercy is the only need.

Break down, O Christ, our heartless faiths,
  And give to us that spirit fine
Which feels in Thee a Comrade strong,
  In every soul a friend of Thine.

THOMAS CURTIS CLARK

*X X Amen* [handwritten]

## The Lost Christ

Where have we laid him now,
This Christ we once so sadly
    placed within a tomb?
So often we have buried him
    safely stowed away, where
    we could come to worship
    and anoint!

*good.* [handwritten]
*The Church conceals rather than reveals Xst often* [handwritten]

We have wrapped him in the trappings
    of the altar,
    and rolled the stone of creed
    against his tomb.
We have dug his grave in busyness
    and repeatedly interred him
    in committee. . . .

*we interp. X* [handwritten]

But always, when we look to find him
    where we laid him,
    the voice of faith proclaims:
"He is not here. He is risen.
He goeth before you!" — *out ahead* [handwritten]

FRANKLIN D. ELMER, JR.

## The Wooden Christ

*Only a symbol to many* [handwritten]

At the high ridge
Of a wide war-stricken realm
There stands an ancient wooden Christ.

Hollow the tottering image towers,
Eyeless and rotten, and decrepit there,
His smile a cruel twist.
Within the empty heart of this old Christ
Small stinging insects build their nests;
And ironhearted soldiers cross themselves
The while they pass
The hollow-hearted figure by.

I think there is no Christ left there
In all those carnage-loving lands
Save only this of hollow wood
With wasp nests
Hiving in its heart.

MARTHA FOOTE CROW

## Hymn to the Perfect

Before Thy cross, O Saviour, we confess
With shame the jangling sin of ugliness,
And pray Thy radiant power will overcome
The dark and dirty alley, street and slum.

For beauty did not leave Thee when life went,
But wrapped Thee in a glowing cerement,
And bore Thee tenderly from breath to breath,
Across the stagnant interlude of death. *until resurre*

EDITH LOVEJOY PIERCE

*But is it stagnant ?*

## The Image in the Forum

Not Baal, but Christus-Jingo! Heir
  Of him who once was crucified!
The red stigmata still are there,
  The crimson spear-wounds in the side;
But raised aloft as God and Lord,
He holds the Money-bag and Sword.

See, underneath the Crown of Thorn,
  The eye-balls fierce, the features grim!
And merrily from night to morn
  We chant his praise and worship him—
Great Christus-Jingo, at whose feet
Christian and Jew and Atheist meet!

A wondrous god! most fit for those
  Who cheat on 'Change, then creep to prayer;
Blood on his heavenly altar flows,
  Hell's burning incense fills the air,
And Death attests in street and lane
The hideous glory of his reign.

O gentle Jew, from age to age
  Walking the waves Thou could'st not tame,
This god hath ta'en Thy heritage,
  And stolen Thy sweet and stainless Name!
To him we crawl and bend the knee,
Naming Thy Name, but scorning Thee!

ROBERT BUCHANAN

## The Lost Christ

Your skill has fashioned stately creeds,
 But where is he, we pray—
The friendly Christ of loving deeds?
 He is not here today.

With sentences that twist and tease,
 Confusing mind and heart,
You forge your wordy homilies
 And bid us heed your art.

But where is he—or can you tell?—
 Who stilled the brothers' strife,
Who urged the woman at the well
 To live a better life?

Where is the Saint of Galilee,
 Crude Peter's faithful guide;
The man who wept at Bethany
 Because his friend had died?

We weary of your musty lore
 Behind dead walls of gray;
We want his loving words once more
 By some Emmaus way.

Give us the Christ who can bestow
 Some comfort-thought of death.
Give us a Christ our hearts can know—
 The Man of Nazareth.

THOMAS CURTIS CLARK

## Passover

But wine was cheap in old Judea. And bread—
Who cared for crumbs except, perhaps, some lone,
Poor, hungry Lazarus, who received a stone?
And who cared for a weary, thorn-bruised head?
Kisses were cheap in dark Gethsemane,
And Roman money hid the light of love
As a penny hides the blazing sun above,
As a moment's fear hides all eternity.

But blood for silver still we sell today,
And we pierce sides and crush poor limbs the same;
Our ritual-kisses true love's task betray,
And yet we dare to mutter, "In His Name"?
O Christ, pass on to some new Calvary—
We, too, have sold and mocked and murdered Thee!

JOHN BEAUCHAMP THOMPSON

## Christ in the Andes

High on the rim edge of the Argentine
The trail to Chile climbs and passes through
White peaks that lift in prayer against the blue
Metallic sky; and here the Nazarene,
A hermitage unto the homeless, stands
Among earth's awful monuments, beside
His cross of Calvary, the ageless guide
To passing pilgrims out of many lands.

He too is pilgrim, walking roads again
In Galilee and Oberammergau;
And everywhere, even today as then,
He wears a wreath of thorn upon his brow,
And whispers in a knowing voice to men
His simple words the world needs sadly now.

CARL JOHN BOSTELMANN

### Refreshment

Forever we are eating up Thy bread,
O Lamb of God; forever drink Thy wine.
Yet ever failing, must bow down the head
In deep humility; our hearts incline
To gain new pardon: "Now go forth again,
O Knights armed only with my victory
Over a world of brash and violent men,
For I go with you, and eternally!"
Would God men were not so—and yet are so!
Ah, Christ! We stab Thee with a thousand sins!
Would do Thy will, yet go as all men go
Down Time's offensive hall of guilty grins
To that dark gate where, in joyful-humble fear,
We beg, "Lord, how may such as I pass here?"

GEORGE EDWARD HOFFMAN

### Christ in the Street

He came to earth one blue-skied day—
  He walked with world-men down the street:
The people stared in a wide-eyed way,
  Noting his wounded hands and feet.

Then they whispered and hurried by:
  Some of them mockingly jibed and smiled
When he stopped where buildings towered high
  To stroke the head of a ragged child.

"Out of the way," the world-men cried;
  "Hurry along," called one in blue:
"You look like a man we crucified,
  "But no . . . Oh, no . . . it was not you!"

"Have you the price of board and bed?"
  They hurled at him as nightfall neared,
And when he shook his thorn-scourged head
  The mob pressed close and laughed and jeered.

"Have you a house of bricks?" they called,
  "Or a chariot which runs alone—
A vault for silver, steeled and walled
  With blocks of mighty granite stone?"

"Have you some other earth-made thing—
  A purse of coins or flying plane?
You who have called yourself a king—
  You must have prospered through your reign."

The night closed in—none gave a crust:
  I heard the wan Christ groan and say:
"Better my dark tomb in the dust
  Than the world today . . . than men today."

JAY G. SIGMUND

## "And Thou Would'st Not!"

He stood upon a slope of Olivet
Brooding, while, like a monstrous, blazing gem
Set in a sapphire crown, the sun appeared
Above the white brow of Jerusalem—
Jerusalem the beautiful, the proud,
Whose children scorned what he would do for them!

I wonder if again today he stands
On some ethereal slope where moonbeams cling,
Gazing upon earth's war-torn citadel,
His eyes pain-dulled, his sad lips whispering
The words he uttered centuries ago,
"I would have gathered thee beneath my wing."

WINIFRED STODDARD LEBAR

## Earth Bows to the New Bomb

What power is this released in man's dark night
  Upon the world where blood was sacrificed?
Has earth forgotten him who healed men's sight,
  The power of Selfless Love in One called Christ?

ALINE BADGER CARTER

*[handwritten margin note: Good. He looks over our world like He looked over Jerusalem.]*

## From "If Jesus Came Back Today"

If Jesus came back today
What would the people say?
Would they cheer him and strew the way
With garlands of myrtle and bay
As they did on that distant day
When he came to Jerusalem?
What would America say
If Jesus came back today?

.    .    .    .    .    .    .    .    .    .

We fashion great churches and creeds
But the heart of the people still bleeds
And the poor still rot in their needs.
We display with pride his cross
In the midst of our pagan life
While we hug to our hearts the dross
Of our selfishness and strife.
What sacrifice have we made
To live the love he prayed?
What willing blood have we shed
To do the deeds he said?
To be popular and well fed
We forsake the way he led
And follow a ghost instead!

VINCENT GODFREY BURNS

### The Jericho Road

I know the road to Jericho,
  It's in a part of town
That's full of factories and filth.
  I've seen the folk go down,

Small folk with roses in their cheeks
  And starlight in their eyes,
And seen them fall among the thieves,
  And heard their helpless cries

When toiling took their roses red
  And robbed them of their stars
And left them pale and almost dead.
  The while, in motor-cars

The priests and levites speeding by
  Read of the latest crimes
In headlines spread in black or red
  Across the "Evening Times."

How hard for those in limousines
  To heal the hurt of man!
It was a slow-paced ass that bore
  The Good Samaritan.
                    EDWIN McNEILL POTEAT

### Thus Speaketh Christ Our Lord
*(Engraved on an old slab in the Cathedral
of Lübeck, Germany)*

Ye call Me Master and obey Me not,
Ye call Me Light and see Me not,
Ye call Me Way and walk not,
Ye call Me Life and desire Me not,
Ye call Me wise and follow Me not,
Ye call Me fair and love Me not,
Ye call Me rich and ask Me not,
Ye call Me eternal and seek Me not,
Ye call Me gracious and trust Me not,
Ye call Me noble and serve Me not,
Ye call Me mighty and honor Me not,
Ye call Me just and fear Me not.
If I condemn you, blame Me not.

ANONYMOUS

### Crowns

Only thorns for the Master,
But bay for the children of men.
The world rolls faster and faster,
Yet Time repeats it again:
A crown of thorns for the Master,
And bay for the children of men.

LOUISE UPHAM BROOKS

### Desert Wanderings

Yes, we have lost our way. No guiding star
Illumes the crooked path that lures afar—
But to what end? To some grim wilderness
Or desert waste which savage beasts possess;
Some stony height, some grim, engulfing sea.
This path is ours to follow, wearily!
But is there no sure road that leads through day?
Is there for us no Guide who knows the way,
A Friend whom we can trust? Still must we grope—
How blindly!—through the waste, and without hope?
In ancient times there walked two lonely men—
Like unto us—Emmaus-ward; and then
Beside them, sudden, walked a Comrade strong.
Is there no Guide for us? O Lord, how long?

THOMAS CURTIS CLARK

### Walls

O Christ, they took Your living words
   And made from them a creed;
They built theology upon
   The words You meant to lead
Men through their darkness and their doubt
   Into a perfect light;
They made great walls that shut You out,
   And only shut in—night!

MYRIAM PAGE

## The Christ

The rumble of distant thunder
rolled from the hills when on the mount
You flung your gauntlet into the crushed faces
and bleeding souls of a thousand years ago.

Now men in cushioned church pews sing
of Christ, the refuge from the world . . .
and few hear the thunder through
the droning of the rain.

EDGAR WILLIAM WHAN

## Was It for This?

Was it for this? The silence and the snow,
The glistening star, the golden angel voices?
Was it for this, two thousand years ago,
The heart, remembering, listens and rejoices?
Men are as cruel, as selfish and as blind
As they were then. And was he born in vain
That life should be a testimony signed
By fingers dipped in blood and scrawled in pain?
Was it for this in silent, white December
We light a Christmas taper and remember?

RENE VERLON

## Certainties

In all his life and teaching
  But two sure things we find,
Two certainties far-reaching:
  He suffered and was kind.

The wounded Christs are falling
  In village and in street
Of miseries appalling,
  With bleeding hearts and feet.

"Where is the kindly Jesus,"
  Their anguished voices say,
"Whose healing touch will ease us
  And take our grief away?"

KENNETH W. PORTER

## Today

The pagan gods of force reclaim their altars,
  The kings of blood again set up their thrones.
In these sad days 'tis only Christ that falters:
  He finds no churches—only splendid stones.

THOMAS CURTIS CLARK

### Meditation in St. Mary's

Do gold-tongued candles comfort Thee
Who tasted darkness on a tree?
Can altar lilies drain
Thy side of pain?
Does perfumed prayer
Thy hands repair,
Or swiftly taken bread
Ease Thy thornèd head, Jesu?

GERTRUDE DU BOIS

*liturgy*

### By an Ancient Sea

Here, on this sunny shore, in simpler days
A Wise Man walked, communing with his friends.
He loved these quiet waters, and the flowers
That flecked those fields with blue and gold. What hours
Of thoughtful talk were theirs—of him who sends
Earth's summer beauty; of the varied ways
Of human life; and of the life to be.
They understood his words—those simple men;
No futile argument or sophistry
Ensnared and vexed their minds. Oh, that again
This Man might talk to us, and know our needs!
Alas, his voice is drowned by jangling creeds!

THOMAS CURTIS CLARK

*creeds vs. needs.*

### If He Should Come

If Jesus should tramp the streets tonight,
  Storm-beaten and hungry for bread,
Seeking a room and a candle light
  And a clean though humble bed,
Who would welcome the Workman in,
  Though he came with panting breath,
His hands all bruised and his garments thin—
  This Workman from Nazareth?

Would rich folk hurry to bind his bruise
  And shelter his stricken form?
Would they take God in with his muddy shoes
  Out of the pitiless storm?
Are they not too busy wreathing their flowers
  Or heaping their golden store—
Too busy chasing the bubble hours
  For the poor man's God at the door?

And if he should come where churchmen bow,
  Forgetting the greater sin,
Would he pause with a light on his wounded brow,
  Would he turn and enter in?
And what would he think of their creeds so dim,
  Of their weak, uplifted hands,
Of their selfish prayers going up to him
  Out of a thousand lands?

                    EDWIN MARKHAM

# The Triumphant Christ

# The Triumphant Christ

## From "In Memoriam"

Strong Son of God, immortal Love,
  Whom we, that have not seen thy face,
  By faith, and faith alone, embrace,
Believing where we cannot prove;

Thine are these orbs of light and shade;
  Thou madest Life in man and brute;
  Thou madest Death; and lo, thy foot
Is on the skull which thou hast made.

Thou wilt not leave us in the dust:
  Thou madest man, he knows not why,
  He thinks he was not made to die;
And Thou hast made him: thou art just.

335

Thou seemest human and divine,
  The highest, holiest manhood, thou.
    Our wills are ours, we know not how;
  Our wills are ours, to make them thine.

ALFRED TENNYSON

### From "Our Master"

We may not climb the heavenly steeps
  To bring the Lord Christ down;
In vain we search the lowest deeps,
  For Him no depths can drown.

. . . . . . . . .

But warm, sweet, tender, even yet
  A present help is He;
And faith has still its Olivet
  And love its Galilee.

The healing of His seamless dress
  Is by our beds of pain;
We touch Him in life's throng and press,
  And we are whole again.

Through Him the first fond prayers are said
  Our lips of childhood frame,
The last low whispers of our dead
  Are burdened with His name.

Our Lord and Master of us all!
  Whate'er our name or sign,
We own Thy sway, we hear Thy call,
  We test our lives by Thine.

JOHN GREENLEAF WHITTIER

### From "Coplas de Manrique"

To One alone my thoughts arise,
The Eternal Truth,—the Good and Wise—
To Him I cry,
Who shared on earth our common lot,
But the world comprehended not
His deity.

HENRY WADSWORTH LONGFELLOW

### Master Musician

He plays across the centuries
    And would from mankind draw the best
With song that has no theme of ease
    But brings the listening spirit rest.

His exquisite insistence pleads
    With deafened souls that stand apart;
The Hand that bows still often bleeds
    When Christ plays vainly on the heart.

MARGARET EVELYN SINGLETON

## "His Is the Way"

The centuries, since Christ to earthland came,
    Have been aflame
    With his fair Name.

The nations that have fallen in decay
    In sad tones say,
    "His is the Way."

And in this age of turbulence and blight,
    Out from the night
    Shines clear his Light.

                  THOMAS CURTIS CLARK

## From "The Over-Heart"

The world sits at the feet of Christ,
    Unknowing, blind and unconsoled;
    It yet shall touch His garment's fold,
And feel the heavenly Alchemist
    Transform its very dust to gold.

              JOHN GREENLEAF WHITTIER

*the hope of universalism*

## The Way, the Truth, and the Life

O thou great Friend to all the sons of men,
Who once appear'dst in humblest guise below,
Sin to rebuke, to break the captive's chain,
To call thy brethren forth from want and woe!—

Thee would I sing. Thy truth is still the light
Which guides the nations groping on their way,
Stumbling and falling in disastrous night,
Yet hoping ever for the perfect day.

Yes; thou art still the life; thou art the way
The holiest know,—light, life, and way of heaven;
And they who dearest hope and deepest pray
Toil by the truth, life, way that thou hast given;
And in thy name aspiring mortals trust
To uplift their bleeding brothers rescued from the dust.

THEODORE PARKER

## O Sun of Life

O Sun of life, O wondrous shining Light,
How pale our candles, flickering in the night!
And yet we boast the splendor of their rays!
Oh, make us humble, Lightener of our days.

O Source of truth, O Wisdom past compare,
Speak unto us, that we Thy truth may share.
May some small portion of Thy heavenly lore
Leaven our minds. Instruct us evermore.

O Heart of God, O great unselfish Love, )
That came to earth, a Father's care to prove,
We have but Thee; there is no other way
To truth, to life, to God's eternal day.

THOMAS CURTIS CLARK

## Not Thou From Us!

Not Thou from us, O Lord, but we
Withdraw ourselves from Thee.
   When we are dark and dead,
And Thou art covered with a cloud,
Hanging before Thee, like a shroud,
So that our prayer can find no way,
Oh! teach us that we do not say,
   "Where is *Thy* brightness fled?"

But that we search and try
What in ourselves hath wrought the blame;
For Thou remainest still the same,
But earth's own vapors earth may fill
With darkness and thick clouds, while still
   The sun is in the sky.
                    RICHARD CHEVENIX TRENCH

## Sovereignty

How soon a mighty throne can fall,
A scepter be forsworn,
A jewel-encrusted diadem
And ermine robe be shorn
Of sovereignty! . . . Yet still remains
A Crown of thorn.
                    LESLIE SAVAGE CLARK

*good or eternal security? He would not let us go?*

## The Disciple

I could not leave Thee, Christ! For when I tried
To leave Thee for alluring ways aside
From Thine own way, Thy power withheld me, kept
My feet from wandering too far, inept
And aimless, down a dwindling path that led
Through mazed confusion to the house of dread.

I could not leave Thee, Christ! For when I yearned
With passionate intensity and burned
With fiery torment to assuage my thirst
For freedom by a turbid stream that burst
In gushing torrents from a naked hill—
Thou ledst me back to waters deep and still.

I could not leave Thee, Christ! For when I sought
To fling aside Thy counsel, when I thought
That in my crazy freedom I should find
Some way of life for body, soul and mind
Better than Thou didst teach, I heard Thee say,
"Come back to Me, for thou hast lost thy way."

I would not leave Thee, Christ! For I am lame
From wandering, and the consuming flame
Of passion has gone out and left my soul
A smoldering ember, and the criss-crossed scroll
Of life ends as it started with the line,
"I cannot leave Thee, Christ! For I am Thine."

DWIGHT BRADLEY

## Search *good — the existential*

Across its wastes a universe I trod—
A cosmos growing greater sun by sun,
A world where light of meaning there was none,
A vast with never voice or face of God.
So, year by year, the weary homeward plod,
The heart-lone, thought-wide search for some high one
Who could with rugged sense the riddle run
Of whence and why: a star—a man—a clod!

And still the dark. And still the search a-grope;
Till one strange day, and in a place unthought,
Lo, dawning Light—a Voice—a Face! Strange hope!
You cannot see? For me it has sufficed
To see all Meaning in the riddle wrought.
Who—Light and Face and Voice? We call him—Christ!

T. MOORE ATKINSON

## Credo

*Not what, but who.*

Not what, but *Whom*, I do believe,
   That, in my darkest hour of need,
   Hath comfort that no mortal creed
   To mortal man may give;—
Not what, but *Whom!*
   For Christ is more than all the creeds,
   And his full life of gentle deeds
   Shall all the creeds outlive.

Not what I do believe, but *Whom!*
   *Who* walks beside me in the gloom?
   *Who* shares the burden wearisome?
   *Who* all the dim way doth illume,
   And bids me look beyond the tomb
   The larger life to live?—
Not what I do believe,
   But *Whom!*
   Not what
   But *Whom!*

JOHN OXENHAM

### The Architect

I would not call him in, my heart decried
The use of any plans except my own;
By them I reared and ceiled four walls of stone.
As blindly too I shut myself inside.
No door was there, no casement opening wide
On darkness such as I had never known:
Imprisoned and discouraged and alone
I knelt amid the ruins of my pride.

And then he came, the Architect Divine,
In tenderness surpassing all my dreams.
"I am the Light," he said, "I am the Door!"
On that I built anew this house of mine;
My walls became his windows, through them streams
The sunlight of his presence more and more.

MOLLY ANDERSON HALEY

## Brothers of the Faith

In Christ there is no East or West,
  In him no South or North;
But one great fellowship of love
  Throughout the whole wide earth.

In him shall true hearts everywhere
  Their high communion find;
His service is the golden cord
  Close binding all mankind.

Join hands, then, brothers of the faith,
  Whate'er your race may be;
Who serves my Father as a son
  Is surely kin to me.

In Christ now meet both East and West,
  In him meet South and North;
All Christly souls are one in him
  Throughout the whole wide earth.

JOHN OXENHAM

## From "The Ring and the Book"

        No one ever plucked
A rag even, from the body of the Lord,
To wear and mock with, but despite himself
He looked the greater and was the better.

ROBERT BROWNING

## On Syrian Hills

It is said the Bedouins cry, on the Syrian hills, a clear
Loud summons to War, and the tribes far distant hearken
  and hear,
So wondrous rare is the air, so crystal the atmosphere.
Their call is to arms; but One, in the centuries long ago,
Spake there for Peace, in tones that were marvelous sweet
  and low,
And the ages they hear him yet, and his voice do the na-
  tions know.

RICHARD BURTON

## The Eternal Word

In the beginning was the Word;
 Athwart the Chaos, night;
It gleamed with quick creative power
 And there was life and light.

Thy Word, O God, is living yet
 Amid earth's restless strife,
New harmony creating still
 And ever higher life.

O Word that broke the stillness first,
 Sound on, and never cease
Till all earth's darkness be made light,
 And all her discord peace.

Till selfish passion, strife and wrong,
    Thy summons shall have heard,
And Thy creation be complete,
    O Thou Eternal Word.

           HENRY WADSWORTH LONGFELLOW

## Prayer

Lord, grant us eyes to see, and ears to hear,
And souls to love, and minds to understand,
And confidence of hope, and filial fear. . . .
Lord, grant us what Thou wilt, and what Thou wilt
Deny, and fold us in Thy peaceful fold;
Not as the world gives, give to us Thine own;
Inbuild us where Jerusalem is built
With walls of jasper, and with streets of gold,
And Thou, Thyself, Lord Christ, the corner-stone.

           CHRISTINA G. ROSSETTI

## From "A Death in the Desert"

I say, the acknowledgment of God in Christ
Accepted by thy reason, solves for thee
All questions in the earth and out of it, . . .

           ROBERT BROWNING

### For God So Loved the World

"For God so loved the world he gave his Son
That all believing on him might have life."
The resurrection morn, God's victory won,
Gleams high above the carnage and the strife
To say to souls distraught and wracked with pain,
To multitudes that watch in darkest night:
"Think not, O world, the Lord Christ died in vain.
He lives to save, to lift men to the light."

For God so loved the world he gave his Son
To bring eternity to death-bound earth,
To win the souls of men to dwell as one
In peace and fellowship, good will and mirth.
This day let Christ be risen in my heart,
That I may see Thee, Father, as Thou art.

GEORGIA HARKNESS

### From "The Descent From the Cross"

Is this the face that thrills with awe
    Seraphs who veil their face above?
Is this the face without a flaw,
    The face that is the face of love?
Yea, this defaced, a lifeless clod,
    Hath all creation's love sufficed,
Hath satisfied the love of God,
    This face, the face of Jesus Christ.

CHRISTINA G. ROSSETTI

### From Epilogue to "Dramatis Personae"

That one Face, far from vanish, rather grows,
Or decomposes but to recompose,
Becomes my universe that feels and knows!

ROBERT BROWNING

*one of the best poems I know, Memorize it*

### The Damascus Road

O sacred lance that heals the wound it makes,
    I bare my heart to thy subduing thrust;
I hail the fear whose rod my faith awakes,
    And deep despair that blossoms into trust.

Did I, my Lord, spurn Thy pursuing quest?
    I grieved the grace that would redeem my loss;
What bliss to know Thy goads incite my rest,
    Find my defeat is victory on the cross.

*"a boundar"*

What can I do now I am all undone?
    My fateful bonds a freer service bring;
What scenes my blindness views beneath Thy sun:
    Lo! I am wounded to release my wing.

Henceforth, dear Lord, do as Thou wilt with me,
    But ever grant a conquering slave's employ;
Be Thou the exile's home on land and sea,
    And tears of love my sacrament of joy.

DANIEL HUGHES

## A Creed

Here is the Truth in a little creed,
    Enough for all the roads we go:
In Love is all the law we need,
    In Christ is all the God we know.

EDWIN MARKHAM

## Christ's Reign of Peace

And he shall charm and soothe, and breathe and bless,
The roaring of war shall cease upon the air,
Falling of tears and all the voices of sorrow,
And he shall take the terror from the grave.

And he shall still that old sob of the sea,
And heal the unhappy fancies of the wind,
And turn the moon from all that hopeless quest;
Trees without care shall blossom, and all the fields
Shall without labor unto harvest come.

STEPHEN PHILLIPS

## A Knight of Bethlehem

There was a Knight of Bethlehem
Whose wealth was tears and sorrows;
His men-at-arms were little lambs,
His Trumpeters were sparrows;

His castle was a wooden cross,
Whereon He hung so high;
His helmet was a crown of thorns
Whose crest did touch the sky.

HENRY NEVILLE MAUGHAN

## The Conquerors

I saw the Conquerors riding by
   With trampling feet of horse and men;
Empire on empire like the tide
   Flooded the world and ebbed again.

A thousand banners caught the sun,
   And cities smoked along the plain,
And laden down with silk and gold
   And heaped-up pillage groaned the wain.

I saw the Conquerors riding by,
   Splashing through loathsome floods of war—
The Crescent leaning o'er its hosts,
   And the barbaric scimitar—

And continents of moving spears,
   And storms of arrows in the sky,
And all the instruments sought out
   By cunning men that men may die!

I saw the Conquerors riding by
   With cruel lips and faces wan:
Musing on kingdoms sacked and burned
   There rode the Mongol Genghis Khan;

And Alexander, like a god,
  Who sought to weld the world in one;
And Caesar with his laurel wreath;
  And like a thing from Hell, the Hun;

And leading, like a star, the van,
  Heedless of upstretched arm and groan,
Inscrutable Napoleon went
  Dreaming of empire, and alone . . .

Then all they perished from the earth
  As fleeting shadows from a glass,
And, conquering down the centuries,
  Came Christ, the Swordless, on an ass!

HARRY KEMP

## The Captains of the Years

I watched the Captains
  A-riding, riding
  Down the years;
The men of mystic grip
  Of soul, a-riding
Between a hedge of spears.

I saw their banners
  A-floating, floating
  Over all,
Till each of them had passed,
  And Christ came riding
A donkey lean and small.

I watched the Captains
    A-turning, staring,
    Proud and set,
At Christ a-riding there—
    So calmly riding
The Road men can't forget.

I watched the Captains
    Dismounting, waiting—
    None now led—
The Captains bowing low!
    The Caesars waiting!
While Christ rode on ahead.
            ARTHUR R. MACDOUGALL, JR.

## From "Io Victis"

Speak, History! Who are life's victors?
    Unroll thy long annals and say;
Are they those whom the world calls
    the victors, who won the success of
    a day?
The martyrs, or Nero? The Spartans
    who fell at Thermopylae's tryst,
Or the Persians and Xerxes? Pilate, or
    Christ?
            WILLIAM WETMORE STORY

## The Holiest Among the Mighty

Christ who, being the holiest among the mighty, and the mightiest among the holy, lifted with his pierced hands empires off their hinges and turned the stream of centuries out of its channel, and still governs the ages.

JEAN PAUL RICHTER

## From "Saul"

I believe it! 'Tis thou, God, that givest, 'tis I who receive:
In the first is the last, in Thy will is my power to believe.
All's one gift: Thou canst grant it moreover, as prompt to
   my prayer
As I breathe out this breath, as I open these arms to the
   air.
From Thy will stream the worlds, life and nature, Thy
   dread Sabaoth:
I will?—the mere atoms despise me! Why am I not loth
To look that, even that, in the face too? Why is it I dare
Think but lightly of such impuissance? What stops my
   despair?
This:—'tis not what man Does which exalts him, but what
   man Would do!

See the King—I would help him but cannot, the wishes
　　fall through. *Rom 7*

Could I wrestle to raise him from sorrow, grow poor to
　　enrich,

To fill up his life, starve my own out,—I would; knowing
　　which,

I know that my service is perfect. Oh, speak through me
　　now!

Would I suffer for him that I love? So wouldst Thou—so
　　wilt Thou!

So shall crown Thee the topmost, ineffablest, uttermost
　　crown—

And Thy love fill infinitude wholly, nor leave up nor
　　down, *Eph 1*

One spot for the creature to stand in! It is by no breath,

Turn of eye, wave of hand, that salvation joins issue with
　　death! *No work of ours whatever; all faith*

As Thy Love is discovered almighty, almighty be proved

Thy power, that exists with and for it, of being Beloved!

He who did most, shall bear most; the strongest shall
　　stand the most weak.

'Tis the weakness in strength, that I cry for! my flesh, that
　　I seek

In the Godhead! I seek and I find it. O Saul, it shall be

A Face like my face that receives thee; a Man like to me,

Thou shalt love and be loved by, forever: a Hand like
　　this hand

Shall throw open the gates of new life to thee! See the
　　Christ stand!

　　　　　　　　　　　　　　　ROBERT BROWNING

## The Day Breaks

Man-made laws and doctrines pass;
Statesmanship is withered grass;
They who spake as sovereign gods
Now are mute as lifeless clods:
Some sure voice the world must seek—
Let the gentle Teacher speak!

Thrones are fallen; wisdom rules;
Foolish kings are kingly fools;
Royal pomp, which craved the sun,
Prostrate is as Babylon;
Love has come to power again:
Lo, the Christ stands—let him reign!

Dead shall be each king and czar—
Dead as all the millions are
Whom they slew in fiendish pride,
Slew to swell war's bloody tide:
Righteous God, the past forgive!
Kings are dead: O King Christ, live!

THOMAS CURTIS CLARK

## From "Saint Paul"

Christ, I am Christ's and let the name suffice you;
    Aye, for me, too, it greatly hath sufficed.
Lo, with no winning words would I entice you,    *I Cor I*
    Paul hath no honor and no friend but Christ.

*That's why Xst comes before Paul to me.*

Yea, through life, death, through sorrow and through
    sinning,
  Christ shall suffice me, for He hath sufficed;
Christ is the end, for Christ was the beginning,
  Christ the beginning, for the end is Christ.

FREDERICK W. H. MYERS

## Only One King

In arrogance and vanity
Kings sculpture regal words and creeds
On granite, that posterity
May marvel at their mighty deeds
Of war and conquest; time and rust
Grind these memorials to dust.

Only one King came scorning power,
Walked with the humble of the land
And served mankind his willing hour:
And he wrote only on the sand!

JOHN RICHARD MORELAND

## Bringers of the Hemlock

They thought to kill old Socrates: instead,
  They launched his name on an immortal tide.
Ten million, blotted out, lie stony dead,
  But one Man lived the more because he died.

STANTON A. COBLENTZ

## One Who Dared to Die

When I consider how proud nations fall
Before the scythe of unrelenting fate, *Dan 2*
And how the kings and lords of this earth ball,
In power one day, the next day take the gate;
When I reflect on mighty men that were
Who now are names forgotten, cast to dust,
I breathe a sigh, no more a worshiper
Of fame and pride, for which all mortals lust.
Of Caesar's battles I have had my fill;
Bold Alexander's triumphs stir no more;
Napoleon is but a name and will—
A name now battered, tinged with human gore. .
And then I think of One who dared to die
Upon a cross, whose name now spans the sky. *Phil 2*

THOMAS CURTIS CLARK

## Room for Him! Room!

Children of yesterday, heirs of tomorrow,
What are you weaving? Labor and sorrow?
Look to your looms again: faster and faster
Fly the great shuttles prepared by the Master;
Life's in the loom: Room for it! Room!

Children of yesterday, heirs of tomorrow,
Lighten the labor and sweeten the sorrow;
Now, while the shuttles fly faster and faster,

Up, and be at it. At work with the Master.
He stands at your loom: Room for him! Room!

Children of yesterday, heirs of tomorrow,
Look at your fabric of labor and sorrow,
Seamy and dark with despair and disaster;
Turn it, and lo! the design of the Master.
The Lord's at the loom.
Room for him! Room!

ANONYMOUS

## Kings

("*They perish all, but He remains.*" *Omar Khayyam*)

Who has not marveled at the might of kings
When voyaging down the river of dead years?
What deeds of death to still an hour of fears,
What waste of wealth to gild a moth's frail wings?
A Caesar to the breeze his banner flings,
An Alexander with his bloody spears,
A Herod heedless of the people's tears!
And Rome in ruin while Nero laughs and sings:
Ye actors of a drama, cruel and cold,
Your names are by-words in Love's temple now,
Your pomp and glory but a winding sheet;
Then Christ came scorning regal power and gold
To wear warm blood-drops on a willing brow,
And we, in love, forever kiss His feet.

JOHN RICHARD MORELAND

## There Lived a Man

Great men have lived
In ages gone; with power they ruled the world.
But time is fleet: their banners now are furled,
And who today is grieved?

Now, other men
Have climbed to fame; how proud and sure their power!
But they—how soon!—will spend their little hour,
And be obscured again.

Apart from fame,
There lived a Man to whom mere power was dross;
He did God's will—and died upon the cross—
And earth reveres his name!

THOMAS CURTIS CLARK

## Dies Irae

There were no footprints left upon the waters
    When Jesus walked on Lake Gennesareth.
The unrecorded words His finger penciled
    In dust upon the road are gone like breath.

Yet when the charts and books are all discarded,
    And, dreadful in the dawn, the horn is heard
Above the ended roads, the canceled phrases,
    Behold! the endless Way, the deathless Word!

JAMES L. DUFF

## No Prisoner of Time

Christ was no prisoner of time,
  His truth transcends each age;
His words beyond compare, sublime;
  His life, life's deathless page.
          WILLIAM H. HUDNUT, JR.

## "If I Be Lifted Up"

"Three things there are," said one,
  "That miracles are—
Dawn, and the setting sun
  And a falling star."

"Two things there be," he said,
  "Beyond man's quest:
The white peace of the dead,
  And a heart at rest."

"One only thing," he cried,
  "Draws all men still—
A stark cross standing wide
  On a windy hill."
          E. P. DICKIE

## The Holy Child

He is the Ancient Wisdom of the World,
 The Word Creative, Beautiful and True,
The Nameless of Innumerable Names,
 Ageless forever, yet Forever New.

CHARLES CARROLL ALBERTSON

## White Splendor

Beyond Arcturus and the Pleiades
 What other worlds may turn
Within the orbit God ordains
 No mortal mind can learn.
Yet one white splendor earth has known,
 And earth's, alone, shall be—
His feet upon Judean hills,
 His Voice by Galilee.

LESLIE SAVAGE CLARK

## His Name

He did not come to judge the world, he did not come to
 blame;
He did not only come to seek—it was to save he came:
And when we call him Saviour, then we call him by his
 name.

DORA GREENWELL

### From "Christ's Victorie and Triumph
### in Heaven and Earth"

He is a path, if any be misled;
He is a robe, if any naked be;
If any chance to hunger, he is bread;
If any be a bondman, he is free;
If any be but weak, how strong is he!
To dead men life he is, to sick men, health;
To blind men, sight, and to the needy, wealth;
A pleasure without loss, a treasure without stealth.

GILES FLETCHER

*Christ is
what we
need.
He is what
our need
is.*

*God's provision*

*God in nature and work*

*Excellent poem — on the
nature of miracles today,
Not quite the same, yet not
different from Bible days.*

### Lo, I Am With You Always

Wide fields of corn along the valleys spread;
    The rain and dews mature the swelling vine;
I see the Lord in multiplying bread;
    I see Him turning water into wine;
    I see Him working all the works divine
He wrought when Salemward His steps were led;
    The selfsame miracles around Him shine;
He feeds the famished; He revives the dead;
    He pours the flood of light on darkened eyes;
He chases tears, diseases, fiends away;

His throne is raised upon these orient skies;
His footstool is the pave whereon we pray.
  Ah, tell me not of Christ in Paradise,
For He is all around us here today.

JOHN CHARLES EARLE

### Repentance

Once I prayed to the Lord of Battles—
Bright-helmeted, steel-brandishing, all-conquering;
Once I sought place in the rolling tides of march-
    ing men, colorful, confident;
Once I shouted, amid the blaze of pageantry and
    the blaring of bugles—
On to victory and glory!

Now I sit, meek and repentant, before a wooden
    Cross, at darkened noontide; a Cross holding
    up to heaven earth's greatest loser of battles—
    and its only Conqueror.

THOMAS CURTIS CLARK

### "He That Doeth the Will"

From all vain pomps and shows,
From the pride that overflows,
And the false conceits of men;
From all the narrow rules
And subtleties of Schools,

And the craft of tongue and pen;
Bewildered in its search,
Bewildered with the cry:
( Lo, here! lo, there, the Church!
Poor, sad humanity
Through all the dust and heat
Turns back with bleeding feet,
By the weary road it came,
Unto the simple thought
By the great Master taught,
And that remaineth still:
Not he that repeateth the name,
But he that doeth the will!

HENRY WADSWORTH LONGFELLOW

*faith without works is dead*

## The Song of a Heathen

If Jesus Christ is a man—
    And only a man—I say
That of all mankind I cleave to him,
    And to him will I cleave alway.

If Jesus Christ is a god—
    And the only God—I swear
I will follow Him through heaven and hell,
    The earth, the sea, and the air!

RICHARD WATSON GILDER

## Loyalty Hymn

While nations rage, while empires rock and fall,
　　While hatred burns, and greed and war increase,
With heart and voice we dedicate our all
　　Once more to Thee, O mighty Prince of Peace.

Fast grow abysmal rifts in every land,
　　O'er creed and class, o'er wealth and soil and blood.
Through all the earth, made one in Thee, we stand—
　　Thy Church in its transcendent brotherhood.

Into the soon forgotten past they die,
　　False gods that rise and flourish for a day.
Not so Thy Cross, firm rooted in the sky;
　　Thy words, O Christ, shall never pass away.

While nations rage, while empires rock and fall,
　　While hatred burns, and greed and war increase,
With heart and voice we dedicate our all
　　Once more to Thee, O mighty Prince of Peace.

　　　　　　　　　　EDITH LOVEJOY PIERCE

### From "The Crystal"

But Thee, but Thee, O sovereign Seer of Time,
But Thee, O poet's Poet, wisdom's Tongue,
But Thee, O man's best Man, O love's best Love,
O perfect life in perfect labor writ,
O all men's Comrade, Servant, King, or Priest—
What *if* or *yet*, what mole, what flaw, what lapse,
What least defect or shadow of defect,
What rumor, tattled by an enemy,
Of inference loose, what lack of grace
Even in torture's grasp, or sleep's, or death's—
Oh, what amiss may I forgive in Thee,
Jesus, good Paragon, Thou Crystal Christ?

                        SIDNEY LANIER

# INDEXES

# INDEX OF AUTHORS

# INDEX OF TITLES